T0305138

Islamic Social Finance

STUDIES IN ISLAMIC FINANCE, ACCOUNTING AND GOVERNANCE

Series Editor: Mervyn K. Lewis, *Professor of Banking and Finance, South Australia and Fellow, Academy of the Social Sciences, Australia*

There is a considerable and growing interest both in Muslim countries and in the West surrounding Islamic finance and the Islamic position on accounting and governance. This important new series is designed to enhance understanding of these disciplines and shape the development of thinking about the theory and practice of Islamic finance, accounting and governance.

Edited by one of the leading writers in the field, the series aims to bring together both Muslim and non-Muslim authors and to present a distinctive East–West perspective on these topics. Rigorous and authoritative, it will provide a focal point for new studies that seek to analyse, interpret and resolve issues in finance, accounting and governance with reference to the methodology of Islam.

Titles in the series include:

Islamic Social Finance
Waqf, Endowment, and SMEs

Shafinar Ismail

Professor of Finance, Faculty of Business and Management, Universiti Teknologi MARA Melaka, Malaysia

M. Kabir Hassan

Professor of Finance, Department of Economics and Finance, University of New Orleans, USA

Suharni Rahmat

PhD graduate, Faculty of Technology Management and Technopreneurship, Universiti Teknikal Malaysia Melaka, Malaysia

STUDIES IN ISLAMIC FINANCE, ACCOUNTING AND GOVERNANCE

Edward Elgar
PUBLISHING

Cheltenham, UK • Northampton, MA, USA

Published by
Edward Elgar Publishing Limited
The Lypiatts
15 Lansdown Road
Cheltenham
Glos GL50 2JA
UK

Edward Elgar Publishing, Inc.
William Pratt House
9 Dewey Court
Northampton
Massachusetts 01060
USA

A catalogue record for this book
is available from the British Library

Library of Congress Control Number: 2022948411

This book is available electronically in the **Elgar**online
Economics subject collection
http://dx.doi.org/10.4337/9781803929804

ISBN 978 1 80392 979 8 (cased)
ISBN 978 1 80392 980 4 (eBook)
Printed and bound by CPI Group (UK) Ltd, Croydon, CR0 4YY

Contents

Figures

Tables

Abbreviations

AI	Artificial Intelligence
AIBIM	Association of Islamic Banking and Financial Institutions Malaysia
AMLA	Administration of Muslim Law Act
AMWC	Al-Muhammadi Mosque Waqf Committee
APIF	Awqaf Properties Investment Fund
AWQAF SA	National Awqaf Foundation South Africa
BARMM	Bangsamoro Autonomous Region in Muslim Mindanao
BAZ	Zakat Amil Body
BDA	Big Data Analysis
BEC	Bumiputra Economic Community
BIBF	Bahrain Institute of Banking and Finance
BIMB	Bank Islam Malaysia Berhad
BMA	Bahrain Monetary Agency
BMMB	Bank Muamalat Malaysia Berhad
BMT	Baitul Mal wal Tamwil
BRAC	Bangladesh Rural Advancement Committee's
CC	Charity Commission
CEO	Chief Executive Officer
CSO	Civil Society Organizations
CSP	Cross-Sector Partnership
CWI	Cash Waqf Institution
CWMES-R	Cash Waqf Micro-Enterprise Support Model for Refugees
DDR	Dompet Dhuafa Republika
EPF	Employees Provident Fund
ERM	Enterprise Risk Management
ESG	Environmental, Social and Governance

FAMA	Federal Agricultural Marketing Authority
GAA	General Authority for Awqaf
GDP	Gross Domestic Product
GERD	Gross Expenditure on Research and Development
GGP	Guidelines on Good Practices
GLC	Government Linked Companies
GLIC	Government Linked Investment Companies
HCD	Human Capital Development
HEI	Higher Education Institution
HMC	Harvard Management Centre
ICM	Islamic Capital Market
ICT	Information and Communication Technologies
ICO	Initial Coin Offering
ICWME-I	Integrated Cash Waqf Microenterprise Investment
IEF	Islamic Economic Finance
IICO	International Islamic Charitable Organization
IICSF	Islamic Commercial and Social Finance
IIEM	Indonesia Islamic Economic Masterplan
IIUM	International Islamic University Malaysia
IMIM	Islamic Micro-Investment Model
INCEIF	International Centre for Education in Islamic Finance
INDEF	Institute for Development of Economics and Finance
IoT	Internet of Things
IRCPP	Islamic Religious Council of Pulau Pinang
IsDB	Islamic Development Bank
ISF	Islamic Social Finance
ISRA	International Shari'ah Research Academy
ITC	International Trade Centre
IWB	Indonesian Waqf Board
IWF	Indonesian Waqf Fund
IWV	Indonesia Waqf Venture
JAWHAR	Jabatan Wakaf, Haji dan Zakat
JC	Johor Corporation

KAPF	Kuwait Awqaf Public Foundation
KLSE	Kuala Lumpur Stock Exchange
KPJ	KPJ Healthcare Berhad
KPKT	Ministry of Housing and Local Government
KSA	Kingdom of Saudi Arabia
KWAN	Waqaf An-Nur Clinics
LLL	Lifelong learning
MAIJ	Johor Islamic Religious Council
MAIN	Majlis Agama Islam Negeri
MAINPP	Majlis Agama Islam Negeri Pulau Pinang
MAIWP	Majlis Agama Islam Wilayah Persekutuan
MARDI	Malaysian Agricultural Research and Development Institute
MARSAH	Johor Institute of Islamic Studies and Arabic Language
MASB	Malaysian Accounting Standard Board
MCM	Mosque Committee Member
MCO	Movement Control Order
MinDA	Mindanao Development Authority
MRCC	Muslim Religious Committee Council
MRL	Malay Reserve Land
MUIB	Brunei Islamic Religious Council
MUIS	Islamic Religious Council of Singapore
MWF	Malaysia Waqf Foundation
NCMF	National Commission on Muslim Filipinos
NCD	Non-Communicable disease
NPC	Narathiwat Provincial Court
NPD	Non-Profit Organization
NRP	National Recovery Plan
PCIA	Provincial Committee for Islamic Affairs
PHK	Termination of Employment Relationship
PMDSG	Pondok Modern Darussalam Gontor
PPAM	Program Perumahan Penjawat Awam Malaysia
PSA	Philippine Statistics Authority
PWS	Selangor Waqf Corporation

QHF	Qard al-Hasan Funds
REIT	Real Estate Investment Trust
RPJMN	Medium-term National Development Plan
RMU	Research Management Unit
R&D&C&I	Research, Development, Commercialization, Innovation
SAR	Sekolah Agama Rakyat
SC	Securities Commission Malaysia
SDGs	Sustainable Development Goals
SIC	Subsidized-ijarah Contract
SEWF	Social Enterprise Waqf Fund
SIRC	State Islamic Religious Council
SMEs	Small and Medium Enterprises
SRI	Sustainable and Responsible Investment
STI	Science, Technology and Innovation
SWT	Subhanahu wa ta'ala
TH	Tabung Haji
TNLC	Thai National Land Code
TPB	Theory of Perceived Behavior
TTSB	Tiram Travel Sendirian Berhad
TVET	Technical and Vocational Education and Training
UDA	Urban Development Authority
UN	United Nations
UNDP	United Nations Development Programme
UNGC	United Nations Global Compact
UNHCR	United Nations High Commission for Refugees
UniTP	University Transformation Programme
VBI	Value-Based Intermediation
WANCorp	Waqf An-Nur Corporation Berhad
WFF	Waqf Future Fund
WKB 2030	Shared Prosperity Vision 2030
WSA	Wakaf Setee Aishah
YWM	Yayasan Wakaf Malaysia
ZISWAF	Zakat, Infaq Donations and Waqf

Foreword

The book not only introduces the definitions and practices of waqf but also gives an overview to the reader on the basic knowledge and fundamentals of waqf and how it works.

The book then explains waqf's role in Sustainable Development Goals (SDGs), by giving the example of the Kingdom of Saudi Arabia and the waqf development approach in Malaysia. It also connects the relations between Islamic Social Finance and SDGs that bring balance to the physical, emotional, mental, and spiritual wellbeing of the community in supporting overall economic growth.

A feature of the book is that it highlights the waqf's contributions in many sectors, including education, properties, agriculture, tourism, Islamic Social institutions, the health industry, Real Estate Investment Trust (REIT), and financial technology (Fintech). Next, the waqf practices in the Southeast Asia countries are discussed. It is believed that Southeast Asia is the home to multiracial groups with diverse beliefs and regions where Islam is the majority religion. Sixty percent of the global Muslim population is in Asia, which contains 11 countries in Southeast Asia, with Indonesia having the highest Muslim population followed by Brunei, Malaysia, Singapore, Thailand, the Philippines, Myanmar, Cambodia, East Timor, Vietnam, and Laos.

There is also a focus on waqf development in Malaysia with the aim of explaining how the government of Malaysia plays a significant role in achieving the objective of waqf development. This discussion leads to the waqf application for entrepreneurship activities, involving SMEs. It is interesting to discover how waqf can help SMEs face the challenges due to the COVID-19 pandemic and the possible solutions that SMEs can take concerning waqf application.

MULYA EFFENDI SIREGAR

Former President Commissioner, Bank Syariah Indonesia

Director of Indonesia Banking Development Institute (LPPI)

Foreword

This book sets out to discover the development of waqf in selected Southeast Asia countries, including Malaysia. The uniqueness of this book lies in presenting the traditional institution of waqf in terms of contemporary practice and applications and the presentation of a different approach in every chapter. First, it introduces the definitions of waqf and the practices of waqf. It is important because it gives an overview to the reader on the basic knowledge and fundamentals of waqf and how it works. Next, it highlights the relationship between Sustainable Development Goals (SDGs) and waqf. Chapter 2 briefly explains the 17 goals of the SDGs and shows how SDGs connect with waqf. The chapter emphasizes the discussion of the United Nations Development Programme (UNDP) initiatives in developing countries.

This book is also interesting because it highlights the waqf's contemporary contributions in many sectors, including education, properties, agriculture, tourism, Islamic Social institutions, the health industry, Real Estate Investment Trust (REIT), and financial technology (Fintech). Next, the waqf practices in the selected Southeast Asia countries are presented to show readers how waqf has been implemented in those selected Southeast Asia countries.

In addition, this book also focuses on waqf development in Malaysia with the aim of presenting to the reader how the government of Malaysia plays a significant role in achieving the objective of waqf development. Thus, Chapter 5 lists the objectives of waqf development in Malaysia (through SDGs) and Malaysia's initiatives in developing waqf practices to achieve the waqf objectives. In the next expansion, Malaysia is taking the initiative to develop waqf practices highlighted in the 11th Malaysia Plan (2016–2020), followed by the 12th Malaysia Plan (2021–2025) to empower SMEs' roles. Finally, there is the waqf application for entrepreneurship activities, which focuses on SMEs. It is interesting to discover how waqf can help SMEs face the challenges due to the COVID-19 pandemic and the possible solutions that SMEs can take concerning waqf application.

HABIB AHMED
Sharjah Chair in Islamic Law and Finance
Durham University Business School, UK

Foreword

In the name of Allah, Most Gracious, Most Merciful

Today's global economy, driven largely by liberal capitalism, is shadowed by the fear that the world's wealth will be monopolised by a handful of corporations at the expense of the majority (World Islamic Economic Forum, WIEF, 2014)

This book sets out to discover the development of waqf in selected Southeast Asian countries, including Malaysia. Furthermore, the book does not only delve into the perspectives of waqf in Southeast Asia, but also introduces the fundamental of waqf implementation and development from various aspects. The chapter begins with the waqf scenario, it focuses on the possibility of using any of the waqf frameworks or models to help micro, small, and medium enterprises (henceforth, SMEs). This is very significant as most SMEs were affected during the COVID-19 pandemic; they needed to sustain their operations throughout the pandemic. Many studies find most SMEs have suffered a significant drop in business within one week of the implementation of Movement Control Order (henceforth, MCO).

The role of waqf is deemed vital, especially during the current economic situation especially in most Muslim nations. They are becoming fragile due to lack of good healthcare services, high unemployment rate, the spread of poverty, and low level of food production, among others. Hence, waqf, which has played an instrumental role in addressing a range of socio-economic issues in the Muslim societies of the past, would be very relevant to the socio-economic development at present as well as for the future. Therefore, it is timely to look at how waqf can contribute to the survival of SMEs during and post COVID-19 pandemic. This book is a must read for those who want to see how waqf plays an essential role in the sustainability of the SMEs.

MANSOR IBRAHIM
Deputy President Academic (DPA)
Dean School of Graduate and Professional Studies
INCEIF

Introduction to *Islamic Social Finance*

In the name of Allah, Most Gracious, Most Merciful

This book introduces the reader to a general waqf context and its roles in the contemporary framework. Besides *zakat* and *sadaqah* as a form of endowments, waqf creates a new horizon among the needy, micro-entrepreneur groups, small-medium groups, and entrepreneurs. In another context, waqf does not only support the financial system, but also contributes to Sustainable Development Goals (henceforth, SDGs) in the 2030 Agendas. Thus, another objective is to relate the roles of waqf with the SDGs, its contributions in many sectors, as well as its practices within the Southeast Asia nations, particularly Malaysia. Finally, this book also highlights the existing waqf frameworks that have been utilized in many countries pertaining to entrepreneurships for the benefits of SMEs. In total, there are six chapters in this book.

Due to the importance of exploring the basic knowledge of waqf, Chapter 1 brings the reader into the concept of waqf through its definition as well as the practices of waqf and contemporary waqf. The definitions of waqf from the perspectives of the four eminent Islamic scholars of al-Hanafi, al-Maliki, al-Syafi'e and Hanbali will be presented. The subsequent parts of the chapter present the types of waqf and other related components in waqf terms in which ten stipulations for the creation of waqf are explained as part of the waqf system practices. Finally, Chapter 1 also presents waqf's contemporary meanings.

Chapter 2 highlights the roles of waqf in the SDGs, which is demonstrated through the participation of UNDP collaboration with Saudi Arabia in exercising waqf and helping Indonesia in improving the waqf programme as to achieve a SDG objective – end poverty. Furthermore, waqf as one of the Islamic Social Finances as well as a third sector economy are further discussed in this chapter.

Chapter 3 focuses on how waqf can be diversified into high performing sectors. This chapter compiles the diversification of waqf from the perspectives of education, properties, agriculture, tourism, Islamic finance, the health-related industry, real estate, and the financial technology sector. More interestingly, this chapter presents the significant role of waqf, which is able to cater to many sectors in various ways.

Chapter 4 allows the reader to explore waqf practices in Southeast Asia. More specifically, this chapter discovers the importance of interrelations among the Southeast Asia countries in working together through waqf practices. Thus, waqf practices are capable of being adapted in order to help Muslim communities participate in financial and commercial matters by putting their wealth into circulation across the globe.

Chapter 5 exposes the reader on waqf practices in Malaysia. This chapter introduces the waqf governance in Malaysia, corporate waqf, and waqf development in the 11th Malaysia Plan. The 12th Malaysia Plan is also highlighted to indicate the importance of the waqf agenda in the development of Malaysia in the period of 2021 to 2025. In this chapter, too, this book highlights the many plans that have been addressed by the Malaysian Prime Minister on the roles of waqf in Malaysia, particularly on its entrepreneurial agendas.

In Chapter 6, the potentials of waqf applications in entrepreneurship are presented. Most importantly, it shows how waqf works to boost entrepreneurship activities. A few models and frameworks are presented in this chapter that can be used by many countries and organizations for setting up as well as for the survival of the SMEs. The impacts of COVID-19 on SMEs and the potential of waqf applications to help the SMEs are also demonstrated in this chapter.

The main aim of this book is to share the strategies, achievements, and initiatives of waqf management, particularly for SMEs. It shows how countries, such as Malaysia, make initiatives to enhance its waqf agenda for the benefit of SMEs, which represent more than 90 percent of business establishments in the country. This book is beneficial to academicians, scholars, entrepreneurs, and industry players to understand the roles of waqf in the contemporary world. In addition, this book is also beneficial to neighbouring countries in Asia as it exposes how Southeast Asia countries manage waqf based on their specific contexts. Furthermore, it widely opens the definition of waqf as one of the Islamic Social Finance instruments through SDGs, as well as presenting waqf as a financing method in various sectors. Additionally, the book also shows how waqf can improve economic growth as many Muslim communities still perceive that waqf is merely for religious-related purposes (e.g. building mosques, orphanage houses, or even cemeteries); thus, this book aims to break these conceptions of waqf. In addition, this book introduces how waqf works in different areas and how it benefits all communities, particularly the SMEs. Therefore, this is our effort to clarify a thorough picture of the waqf concept through the elevation of the development of waqf. Even though the book does not specifically highlight waqf-related issues, it provides a substantial insight on views, opinions, and knowledge on waqf management and the success of waqf development in many sectors.

This book is unique because it offers perspectives of waqf from what has been practised in developing countries based on relevant models and frameworks, as well as highlighting the initiatives taken by the Malaysian government to assist the SMEs before, during, and after the COVID-19 pandemic.

Shafinar Ismail
M. Kabir Hassan
Suharni Rahmat

1. The concept of waqf

This chapter introduces the definitions of waqf from the four eminent Muslim scholars. Next, the practices of waqf are discussed including its components, types, ten stipulations, and contemporaries of waqf.

DEFINITIONS OF WAQF

A waqf is an inalienable charitable endowment under Islamic law. It typically involves donating assets for Muslim religious or charitable purposes with no intention of reclaiming those assets. A waqf is an endowment made by a Muslim under Islamic Law to a fund manager who is responsible for generating profits that are subsequently used to support socioeconomic development. A waqf is similar to an endowment fund but is strongly encouraged in Islam as a contribution to society (Sukmana, 2020).

The term waqf (or awqaf) which means stopping, containing, or preserving something, is derived from an Arabic root verb. Waqf in Arabic is literally referred as *al-Habsu 'an at-Tasarruf* which means to hold, keep, or detain. Waqf is also known as *Boniyat* or *Habs*, and these two terms are used primarily in Iran and North Africa, respectively. In other words, waqf means a unique form of endowment by a waqif (donor or endower) who gives up some of his personal assets (for example, in the form of cash) to be used forever or for a certain period of time in accordance with his interests (Husin, 2020).

In legal terms, waqf is defined as a perpetual dedication of a certain property to Allah SWT by devoting the property's benefits to religious and charitable causes (Md Saad et al., 2017). The National Awqaf Foundation of South Africa outlines that, in Shariah, waqf is a voluntary, permanent, irrevocable, cash or kind devotion of one's wealth to Allah SWT. The National Awqaf Foundation of South Africa mentions that once waqf is dedicated, it cannot be changed, confiscated, or sold. It belongs to Allah, and the waqf remains intact at all times. Ismail et al. (2021), quoting from Kahf (1998), states that waqf from a Shariah perspective is 'holding an asset and preventing its use to repeatedly extract its usufruct for the benefit of a noble or philanthropic objective'.

In the context of socio-economics, waqf can be used as a mechanism to increase the standard of living within the *ummah* (society), reduce poverty and difficulties among the poor, and maintain a good living. This is done through a fair wealth distribution among the society members (Salarzahi et al., 2010).

DEFINITIONS OF WAQF BY SCHOLARS

As explained by AlButi (2009), the four eminent Islamic scholars of *al-Hanafi*, *al-Maliki*, *al-Syafi'e* and *Hanbali* have different definitions of waqf, or endowment, as follows (Hasan and Ahmad, 2017).

Al-Hanafi: Waqf is intended to preserve and upkeep the original wealth that belongs to someone else and grants its profits to the needy. By this, we can learn that waqf's purpose is to preserve the wealth or something that can give benefits or profit, without it being consumed by the original owner and the benefits or profit from it are to be bequeathed to the needy. According to Hanafi, through waqf, kindliness is manifested, and it is offered to those in need in the spirit of camaraderie and it this gesture that will be rewarded by God as a good deed on the day of resurrection.

Al-Maliki: Ownership of the profit originated from the wealth given as an endowment is granted to whoever the endowment was meant for or the needy. By this it can be understood that waqf is to give the right to consume the profit of wealth that was given for endowment to whoever the endowment was meant for or the needy. According to Maliki, waqf is an engagement that is recommended (*sunnah*) in Islam.

Al-Syafi'e: Waqf is intended to keep the wealth that can give benefits, maintaining it in the same form, and the original owner is not allowed to consume it. It can be learnt that waqf is to keep the wealth that can give benefits to the needy, and that wealth remains in the same condition while the original owner cannot consume it. According to Syafi'e, it is recommended (*sunnah*) in Islam to keep the benefits of certain wealth and grant its benefit to the needy or people who deserve it.

Hanbali: Waqf is keeping the original owner from consuming wealth that he had endowed to supply benefits to the needy, and the wealth is maintained in the same form. According to Hanbali, waqf is an engagement that is recommended by Islam and can make us nearer to God.

PRACTICES OF WAQF

This section explains the components of waqf, types of waqf, ten stipulations for the creation of waqf and contemporary waqf. Contemporary waqf consists of cash waqf, waqf shares, and corporate waqf.

Waqf Components

There are four major components of any waqf: (1) the Donor or Endower (*waqif*); (2) the Beneficiaries (*mawqūf 'alayh*); (3) the waqf institution or

Table 1.1   Descriptions of waqf's main components

Waqf components	Descriptions
Waqif – The Donor or Endower	A contributor, who decides to give his personal wealth as waqf for a specific purpose
Mawqūf 'alayh – The Beneficiaries	Recipients
Mutawalli – The waqf institution or Trustee	Who oversees the waqf property to the wellbeing of the beneficiaries
Mawquf – The Corpus/endowed property	The original capital (property or cash waqf) given by the waqif is called a *mawquf* (corpus/endowed property)

Trustee (*mutawalli*); and (4) the corpus/endowed property (*mawquf*). A contributor, who decides to give his personal wealth as waqf for a specific purpose is called '*waqif*'. The original capital (property or cash waqf) given by the *waqif* is called '*mawquf*' (corpus/endowed property). *Waqif* strictly specifies how the corpus should be used or spent. Thus, the privately gathered wealth of a devout Muslim turns into God's property. The *waqif* carefully specifies how the yearly income of the waqf should be spent. This income (usufruct) might be dispensed totally for a devout reason, or to a group of recipients (beneficiaries). The administration of the waqf is endowed to waqf institutions or trustees, *mutawalli*, who oversees the waqf *property* to the wellbeing of the *mawqūf 'alayh* (recipients). The main duty of *mutawalli* is to preserve the property and to maximize the revenues of the beneficiaries. Table 1.1 gives descriptions of the waqf's main components.

Types of Waqf

In principle, the classification of waqf can be divided into three types: waqf *khairy*, waqf *ahli,* and waqf *mushtarak.*

First, waqf *khairy* or religious waqf is commonly allocated for mosques and religious schools. Waqf *khairy* is classified into two forms: waqf *mutlak* (general waqf) and waqf *muqayyad* (special waqf). Waqf mutlak refers to the practice of handing over waqf without a specific purpose in waqf state property. The property can be developed for any purpose as long as it does not conflict with Islamic law (Mohamed Nor and Yaakub, 2015). Waqf *Muqayyad* is the waqf of dedicating a property where the donor states the giving of waqf for specific purposes, while dedicating the property and its ownership to be used only for the purpose stated by the *waqif*. The waqf property from waqf *muqayyad* can be endowed in immovable and movable properties. Generally, an immovable property refers to assets such as lands and buildings, while a movable property can be in the form of books, prayer mats, and even cash.

Mohamed Nor and Yaakub (2015) state that a majority of scholars argue that any waqf property that can be traded can be donated while the benefits can be enjoyed by the recipient on an ongoing basis.

The second type of waqf is waqf *ahli*, also known as 'family waqf', which is absolutely created for the interest of house members (inclusive of the founder or *waqif*) or for other persons that the founder specifies (Abdel Mohsin et al., 2016). Husin (2020), quoted from Hennigan (2004), agreed that for waqf *ahli*, if the waqf is in the form of property, its income will be allocated to the heirs and for charitable purposes – in other words, it is for an immediate member of the owner's family. Waqf *ahli*'s advantages are given to such people who have an individual relationship or are associated by ancestry to the benefactor. The beneficiaries of the trust are together the relatives of the first beneficiary. Upon the passing of the named beneficiaries' and founders' relatives, Sait and Lim (2006) mentioned that the waqf properties' endowed advantages will be given to charity with no constraints (Ibrahim and Ibrahim, 2013). Mohamad (2018) explained that the requirements of waqf *ahli* are the same as normal waqf. It requires the fulfillment or compliance with the same principles and conditions as other types of waqf but the benefits of waqf can be specifically allocated to family members to ensure their security in terms of education, future life, and depending on the donor's intentions.

Nevertheless, historically, waqf *ahli* is more popular due to two major reasons. First, waqf *ahli* was formed for the family to retain the properties intact, to guarantee the beneficiaries' rights during the period of the waqf objects, and to govern the transference of property endowed benefits from one generation to another (Husin, 2020). Doumani (1998) added that waqf *ahli* was also seen as the ideal instrument for protecting the family's wealth in countries that are facing frequent political and economic turmoil, as waqf properties cannot be seized either to please the ruling power or to collect amount dues. Second, waqf *ahli* was used to restrict divisions of wealth due to Islamic inheritance jurisprudence (Husin, 2020). Taking the view of other scholars, Mohamad (2018) states that the benefits of waqf *ahli* are sometimes overshadowed by the claim that it is also possible to avoid Islamic inheritance rules and bequeath to certain family members through waqf *ahli*. The claim is in line with the principles of English charitable trust law, where family members are not legally categorized as legal beneficiaries therefore the dedication is void. The effects of colonization in some Islamic countries such as Egypt, Malaysia, and India show that waqf members have been declared invalid, or restrictions have been imposed on waqf before it can be legalized. Nevertheless, waqf *ahli* is no longer popular nowadays. In fact, the creation of waqf *ahli* is restricted in numerous Islamic countries, such as Lebanon, Syria, and Egypt.

Waqf *mushtarak* is a combination of waqf *khairy* and waqf *ahli*. It is also called the philanthropic waqf. Usually, under this type of waqf, the founder (*waqif*) will specify the target beneficiaries (usually family members) and later assign the benefits for broader welfare purposes (Yaacob, 2013). Waqf *mushtarak* is formed to benefit the *waqif* house members as well as for benevolent and public reasons. Siraj (2012) mentions that waqf *mushtarak* is widely practiced in Egypt. Generally, part of the waqf proceeds will be channeled to the founder's preferred mosque, or school, or for certain religious services such as reciting the Qur'an at his tomb, while the other part will go to public beneficiaries. Other examples of beneficiaries are libraries, educational centers, health care, animal care, taking care of the environment, development activities of green spaces, and roads. The existence of waqf mushtarak is hardly traceable in Malaysia (Yaacob, 2013). The next topic will discuss the ten stipulations for the creation of waqf.

Ten Stipulations for the Creation of Waqf

Muslim jurists approved ten stipulations for the creation of waqf. These stipulations give flexibility in switching the revenue of the waqf from one beneficiary to another according to the needs of different societies. These ten stipulations are initially derived from five pairs of stipulations. The first three pairs grant flexibility in terms of changing the mode of distribution of the revenue of the waqf to beneficiaries, while the last two pairs allow actual changes in the waqf property itself (Abdel Mohsin et al., 2016).

(1) *Ziyadah* (increase) and *Nuqsan* (decrease)
This stipulation gives the right to the founder to increase the share of one beneficiary and at the same time to decrease the share of another beneficiary. This is an important condition. If the founder created a waqf in order to distribute its revenue equally to a specific mosque and hospital, and if later he or the trustee realizes that the hospital needs more than 50 percent and the mosque needs less than 50 percent, they can, by virtue of this *ziyadah/nuqsan* stipulation, increase the share of the hospital up to 70 percent and decrease the share of the mosque to up to 30 percent.

(2) *Idkal* (addition) and *Ikhraj* (removal)
This condition gives the founder or the trustee the right to add a new beneficiary if he realizes the need to add a new beneficiary and at the same time remove another beneficiary. This stipulation also gives flexibility to the public waqf by removing a beneficiary whenever the founder 'feels' that there is another beneficiary who is in more need than the first. This means increased flexibility for public services too. For example, directing the revenue of the waqf from building a dam, once the dam is finished, to another important service, such as providing water or electricity supply according to the needs of society.

Table 1.2   Ten stipulations for waqf creation and sustainability

Ten stipulations	Descriptions
Ziyadah (increase) and *nuqsan* (decrease)	Gives the right to the founder to increase the share of one beneficiary and decrease (*nuqsan*) the share of another beneficiary
Idkal (addition) and *Ikhraj* (removal)	Gives the founder/the trustee the right to add a new beneficiary if he realizes the need and remove (*ikhraj*) the beneficiary
I'ta' (granting) and *hirman* (dispossession)	Permits the founder/the trustee to grant all or a portion of his waqf revenue to whomever he chooses for a specified period and to *hirman* (dispossess) whomever he chooses
Taghyir (replacement) and *tabdil* (conversion)	Gives the founder the right to replace the use of waqf revenue (*taghyir*) or, instead of maintaining the waqf property, the founder can purchase other equipment (for example, surgical instruments for a needy hospital)
Istibdal (substitutions) *Ibdal* (purchase)	Purchase of another property to replace (*istibdal*) the former waqf property and actual sale of non-profitable waqf property

(3) *I'ta'* (granting) and *Hirman* (dispossession)

This stipulation permits the founder or trustee to grant all or a portion of his waqf revenue to whomever he chooses for a specified period and to dispossess whomever he chooses. For example, if the revenue of a certain waqf is directed to support a student at a certain university, the founder can grant a portion or all of that revenue to a needier beneficiary, such as to a patient at a certain hospital.

(4) *Taghyiy* (replacement) and *Tabdil* (conversion)

Taghyir gives the founder the right to put the waqf revenue to another preferred use, for example, instead of maintaining the waqf property, the founder can purchase other required equipment, such as surgical instruments for a needy hospital. *Tabdil*, in fact, gives the founder the right to change the waqf property itself. For example, if the founder creates agricultural land as a waqf, and after many years this land becomes unproductive, the *taghir* stipulation gives the founder the right to change its function and perhaps construct a house on it.

(5) *Istibdal* (substitution) and *Ibdal* (exchange)

Ibdal is the actual selling of non-profitable waqf property, while *Istibdal* is the purchase of another property to replace a waqf property. This is an extremely important stipulation, which can be applied by the founder or trustee, with the permission of the chief justice, even if the founder did not include it in his written deed. This stipulation gives the trustee the right to exchange an unprofitable waqf property with another property that is profitable. Table 1.2 simplifies these stipulations.

It is very important to inform new founders about these ten stipulations (particularly the first three) so that they would consider these in their waqf deeds, since, from the Islamic law perspective, if the founder does not include these stipulations in his deeds, the chief judge and the trustee, for example, cannot switch the distribution of waqf revenue to other beneficiaries. The last two stipulations can, however, be affected by the chief judge and trustee with or without prior stipulation by the founder. Hence, including them will give flexibility whenever the need arises within a society or whenever changes in the waqf properties are needed (Abdel Mohsin et al., 2016).

Contemporary Waqf

According to Islamic law, contemporary waqf can be classified as a new product (a form of liquid assets) in addition to existing traditional forms of waqf such as cash waqf, stock waqf, waqf *wakalah*, cooperative waqf, and hybrid waqf. Contemporary waqf can be expressed as representing the granting of ownership rights to some property that can be used, either in the form of interest or profit can be obtained; profits from real estate; waqf by users, waqf from family members (*waqf al-aulad*), and *waqf al nuqud* (cash waqf). Thus, in this context, contemporary waqf can be defined as current and according to the changes of the new era.

Cash waqf
Cash waqf, or cash endowment, is a form of liquid asset that can be channeled immediately towards certain investment objectives, and the dividends or capital gains derived can be utilized to meet the desired aims under the waqf charter. The cash waqf is usually formed where the pooled donations are used to build institutions, such as schools, hospitals, and orphanages. It is argued that a cash waqf can pool more resources and ensure a wider participation of individual donors.

Husin (2020) expresses that, historically, cash waqf was widely used and contributed considerably to social development during the Ottoman period, to such an extent that education, health care and community welfare were entirely financed by waqf. They further argued that cash waqf functioned mainly as a capital redistribution institution rather than a capital accumulation institution.

From the viewpoint of Deloitte Indonesia (2021), there are four different types of cash waqf that differ based on the motives or intentions of the *waqif*: donation or charity-based; reward-based; equity-based; and lending-based.

In other perspectives, Azganin et al. (2021) defined a cash waqf as a perpetual mobilization of funds from donors to be invested in productive assets that provide revenues or usufruct for future consumption while taking into consideration the guidelines and policies given by donors as well as recipients.

This is known as the conditions of *waqif* (*Shart alWaqif* in Arabic). The most acceptable waqf is a cash waqf, which is an endowment of certain amounts of money for investment, as it is managed by a waqf manager (*Mutawalli*).

A cash waqf, which may be considered as movable property, has led to the innovation and enhancement of the waqf institutions globally. Versions of the concept have emerged in different countries, providing credible evidence of the opportunities that lay ahead in waqf innovation. Abdelfattah et al. (2021) state that cash waqf began in Sudan in 1990, followed by Malaysia, Indonesia, and Kuwait. These countries reinvigorate waqf activities through new schemes to match the needs of growing societies' public services. Below are examples of direct cash waqf and deposit cash waqf.

(a) Direct cash waqf
This is the most popular form of cash waqf. A noteworthy example in practice is what has been done in Singapore for the purpose of assisting orphans, Islamic schools, charity, and the burial of poor Muslims. Another example is the practice in New Zealand for similar groups of beneficiaries. Any dividends from a cash waqf are utilized for Islamic schools, marriage guidance, orphans and other social services for the expat Muslim communities living there. In India, cash waqf is used for those with disabilities, distribution of food during Ramadan, and general support of Muslim communities.

(b) Deposit cash waqf
Selected Islamic banks in Malaysia provide a product facility for the collection of cash waqf through a deposit scheme. Bank Islam Malaysia Berhad, Bank Muamalat Malaysia Berhad and Maybank Islamic Berhad provide a deposit service for the collection of funds to redevelop old waqf properties. In Malaysia, a significant amount of old waqf assets comprise undeveloped lands. There is an urgency for the provision of financing from Islamic banks that would support the development of these assets so that they may finally provide the benefits as intended by the *waqif* (founder). An Islamic bank in Bangladesh also has similar schemes utilizing returns for socially responsible initiatives.

Up to now, the social goods and services typically financed by cash waqf have been in (i) education: schools, both religious and contemporary education; (ii) health sector: primary hospitals but may also include specialist hospitals, e.g., a cancer treatment and research hospital; (iii) orphanages and residential facilities for working women; (iv) interest-free financing for personal use or for setting up small businesses (microfinance); (v) public parks and other public amenities; and (vi) drinking water (Global Islamic Finance Report, 2015).

Thus, cash waqf helps society immensely, from providing basic facilities to the public, including social, health, environmental, education and infrastructures. In devising their economic strategies, many signatory Muslim countries already use cash waqf to support community development in their respective countries and as a tool against poverty (Najim, 2021).

Waqf shares – sukuk

There are different terms between waqf shares and waqf of shares. Waqf shares refer to the creation of a waqf through the issuance of shares which are subsequently endowed as a waqf by the purchaser to the *Majlis*. For example, sukuk. Waqf of shares means the shares of a company or an enterprise or existing shares dedicated for waqf (Global Islamic Finance Report, 2015). The following part discusses the waqf shares in sukuk.

Initially, sukuk are Islamic bonds. The literal meaning of sukuk is certificates. Over the years, sukuk have progressively become the preferred choice for fundraising by public entities and private companies in many jurisdictions seeking a wider market for their funding needs. Due to the additional value-added of social benefits and Islamic principles incorporated into its structure as opposed to the typical conventional bond offering, sukuk would naturally appeal to a broader investor base.

The demand for sukuk comes from investors who seek Shariah-compliant investments such as takaful operators, Shariah-based unit trust funds, Islamic fund managers as well as non-Islamic institutions. The non-Islamic institutions view sukuk as a new asset class that fits their investment strategies and/ or diversifies their portfolios, as the yields are competitive against similar conventional instruments. Since most sukuk are assessed and rated by rating agencies, investors could refer to the sukuk rating as a guideline to assess risk or return parameters of the sukuk issue. Sukuk offers a regular periodic income stream and a possibility of capital appreciation. They are also tradable and allow for easy liquidation, should there be a need for immediate cash.

According to The World Bank Group, INCEIF, and ISRA (2019), sukuk are one of the cash waqf channels developed to modernize waqf in this new era. Sukuk refer to investment certificates that represent ownership in underlying projects. The investors may receive profit or income from the cash flow generated from the assets or investment in the asset in the form of periodic distributions. The returns may be fixed or variable depending on the mechanisms applied. Sukuk are structured based on various Shariah contracts to create financial obligations and relationships between issuers and investors (Securities Commission Malaysia, 2014). This ownership may be directly linked to the underlying asset or to the securitized cash flows of the underlying project. The advantages of applying a sukuk structure include the fact that sukuk are generally rated, have significantly reduced risk and provide consistent returns to investors, similar to conventional bonds.

In general, sukuk could also be used to finance infrastructure projects that become an *awqaf* after the investors have been paid off. In addition, waqf institutions can opt to explore raising capital for the development of their waqf projects through the issuance of sukuk. Sukuk are a widely used instrument in the Islamic capital market to finance specific economic activities in accordance with Shariah principles. Sukuk have flexible characteristics in which they can be structured to meet the medium to long-term financing requirements. Thus, sukuk may be issued for various purposes to satisfy the issuer's commercial needs, such as for the purpose of financing working capital and capital expenditure requirements, vis-à-vis the investors' (sukukholders) investment and risk appetite.

Wakalah waqf

According to Securities Commission Malaysia (2014), wakalah means a contract where a party authorizes another party to act on behalf of the former, based on the agreed terms and conditions as long as he/she is alive.

Abdullah and Yaacob (2012) discuss that wakalah waqf is derived from the model to enhance the channel of takaful products. IGILife (2021) states that, generally, the wakalah waqf model operates through a waqf fund. The participants contribute their contributions on the basis of '*Taburru*' into the waqf fund. The waqf fund is responsible for channeling the fund urgently (in emergency situations) to the needy. At this point, takaful claims are paid through waqf fund. The surplus in waqf fund (if any) is distributed amongst participants at the end of every year.

Corporate waqf

In general, according to Saad (2019), corporate waqf is formed to benefit from one of the six main objectives: business entities or corporations, banking and financial institutions, universities, foundations, cooperatives, and hospitals or clinics.

This section presents the definitions of corporate waqf through scholars' views. First, Omar et al. (2018) exemplify corporate waqf as liquid money, shares, profit, and dividends that have been declared as waqf by the corporate sector with the aim of distributing the benefits derived from the stock dividend and the company's annual profit. Saad (2019) mentions that, in some cases, the corporate waqf is the majority owner of a company and exercises managerial control, while in other cases the corporate waqf is the minority shareholder and exercises minority voting rights. In another view, corporate waqf is also known as contemporary waqf, and has been practiced in many countries, namely Turkey, Malaysia, India, Pakistan, and Bangladesh (Omar et al., 2018).

There are many types of corporate waqf that can be practiced. First, as mentioned by Saad (2019), there is the example of institutions whose asset base is comprised of shares in a company and who hold some managerial roles in that company. The corporate waqf's share in a company ranges from a minority percentage to complete ownership. The corporate waqf is established by a company's founder, individual shareholders, or government entities. Governmental regulation ranges from exercising complete control over the waqf assets to providing limited oversight by the trustees to prevent managerial abuse. Some core features are consistently observed across the various corporate waqf: the perpetual nature of the foundation, divestment of ownership from the original shareholder, the management of the endowed shares by a not-for-profit entity, and the allocation of returns to a charitable foundation. Similarly, Jalil and Mohd Ramli (2014) state that the corporate entity will create its own waqf assets using its own assets. In this situation, the corporate entity is the waqf creator or '*al-waqif*' itself. The waqf assets could be financial assets, such as cash or shares or non-financial assets such as buildings or lands. At the same time, the corporate entity nominates itself as the trustee who is responsible for managing, maintaining, and investing the waqf asset. This means that the corporate entity is also the '*nazir*' or '*mutawalli*' of the waqf asset.

Although different versions exist, Saad (2019) mentions that corporate waqf is most widely practiced in Turkey, Malaysia, India, Pakistan, and Oman. In Oman, for example, some private property developers assign a portion of the property, say 20 percent, for the purpose of waqf. This means that all rental from the assigned waqf would be channeled to the beneficiaries for educational scholarships, microfinance programs, and other initiatives.

The corporate waqf has its own legal rights and liabilities to carry out the jobs of the founder(s), as a trust, and to conduct a business on their behalf for either profit-seeking or not-for-profit in order to benefit society at large. In addition, due to its legal personality, once it is registered it will have a condition of limited liability. It is where the founders' conditions need to be respected, fulfilled and controlled by a board of directors which was appointed by the founders (Abdel Mohsin, 2013).

Waqf can be translated as a unique form of endowment by a *waqif* (donor or endower) who gives up some of his personal assets (for example, in the form of cash) to benefit others forever or for a certain period of time in accordance with their interests.

WAQF IN ISLAMIC ECONOMIC DEVELOPMENT

Many believe that the waqf system is not a new affinity for modern Islamic economics. Since the eighth century, most Muslim-dominated states have provided a large scale of public goods to their respective countries. These widespread resources flow to the waqf and result in many services being financed through waqf, including mosques, schools, hospitals, fountains, roads, parks, accommodations, bathhouses, orphanages, and soup kitchens. For instance, waqf's services to big cities in the Middle East have been established for a long time. Waqf is a fundamental economic institution that generates economic activities while simultaneously ensuring benefits to a particular part of society (Budiman, 2014).

Cizakca (1998) states that this waqf system can contribute to the modern economy. Obviously, waqf is not part of government expenditure. Indeed, the waqf system has been applied to various essential services – such as health, education, municipalities, land, building, and many more, which have been made available in history at no cost to the government. This happened with individual or private sector involvement. The waqf system encourages individual or private sector participation via their voluntary actions and automatically reduces government involvement in the economy. The more waqf funds are collected for specific development projects that benefit the community, the less the government will be involved in particular projects (Ismail et al., 2021).

Waqf has played a particular function in the economic aspect and always has potential. Waqf could be regarded as a fundamental economic institution to generate economic activities while at the same time ensuring that the benefits will accrue to a certain part of society. In an economic sense, waqf could be defined as diverting funds and other resources from current consumption and investing them into productive and prospective assets that generate revenues for future consumption by individuals or society at large. Waqf is, therefore, a peculiar combination between the act of saving and the act of investing. It operates by taking specific resources off consumption and simultaneously putting them in the form of productive assets that increase capital accumulation in the economy. The waqf implies sacrificing a current consumption opportunity for the benevolent purpose of providing income and services for society and the following generations.

In line with the principle of perpetuity in waqf, a waqf asset may not be sold or disposed of. It should remain in the waqf domain perpetually. Should there be a new waqf, it will be added to that domain. Therefore, waqf assets will continually increase. At the same time, they are not permitted to decline due to the prohibition on consuming the assets of waqf or leaving them idle by any action or neglect or transgression. Hence, waqf is not only an investment, but it is a cumulative and increasing investment. This is supported by the historical development of Muslim lands. The extent of waqf properties was estimated to be over one-third of the agricultural land in several countries, including Turkey, Morocco, Egypt, and Syria. The dynamism of the waqf institution and its mechanism could bring about essential contributions to economic development at the present time.

The next chapter will explain how waqf can be practiced and implemented, and be sustained in contributing towards economic development.

2.   The role of waqf in sustainable economic development

It is said that waqf can enhance long-term investments, but little tells us how waqf can be sustained. Waqf has the potential to contribute to long-term economic development and, regarding this potential, Islamic Development Bank Group president, Dr. Ahmed Mohamed Ali mentioned that the joint initiative of the Islamic Development Bank Group and the World Bank Group benefits to overcome the widening global wealth gap. This is where the role of Islamic finance supports this problem, and aligns with the Sustainable Development Goals (SDG), with a focus on ending poverty, fighting inequality and injustice, and tackling climate change by 2030. The Islamic Development Bank Group, in its 2016–2025 Strategic Plan, gives priority to inclusive and sustainable socio-economic development among member countries within its role in advancing Islamic finance globally. Besides imposing social and environmental costs, severe inequality adversely affects economic growth and wealth creation. The question that needs to be addressed is how to minimize the disparity in wealth and enhance shared prosperity. Given its potential role in economic development, Islamic finance can contribute to achieving these objectives.

This chapter accentuates the relationship between SDGs and waqf. Ending poverty is one of the criteria that is attracting attention in relation to SDGs and waqf plans. The relations between SDGs and waqf are presented in achievement and development forms. First, this chapter briefly explains the 17 goals of the SDGs and shows how SDGs connect with waqf, followed by the participation of the government in managing waqf practices. Next, the discussion is about the participation of the United Nation Development Programme (UNDP) initiatives in developing countries, including the waqf development approach in Malaysia. Finally, the roles of waqf in the third-sector economy are presented.

SUSTAINABLE DEVELOPMENT GOALS IN THE 2030 AGENDA

Sustainable Development Goals are the 2030's core agenda, with 17 goals and 169 targets. The 2030 Agenda is a new approach by United Nations (UN) to achieve a global commitment towards more sustainable, resilient, and inclu-

Table 2.1   *Sustainable Development Goals based on the 2030 Agenda*

Goals	Agenda
1	End poverty in all its forms everywhere
2	End hunger, achieve food security and improved nutrition, and promote sustainable agriculture
3	Ensure healthy lives and promote well-being for all at all ages
4	Ensure inclusive and equitable quality education and promote lifelong learning opportunities for all
5	Achieve gender equality and empower all women and girls
6	Ensure availability and sustainable management of water and sanitation for all
7	Ensure access to affordable, reliable, sustainable, and modern energy for all
8	Promote sustained, inclusive, and sustainable economic growth, full and productive employment and decent work for all
9	Build resilient infrastructure, promote inclusive and sustainable industrialization, and foster innovation
10	Reduce inequality within and among countries
11	Make cities and human settlements inclusive, safe, resilient, and sustainable
12	Ensure sustainable consumption and production patterns
13	Take urgent action to combat climate change and its impacts
14	Conserve and sustainably use the oceans, seas and marine resources for sustainable development
15	Protect, restore and promote sustainable use of terrestrial ecosystems, sustainably manage forests, combat desertification, and halt and reverse land degradation and halt biodiversity loss
16	Promote peaceful and inclusive societies for sustainable development, provide access to justice for all and build effective, accountable and inclusive institutions at all levels
17	Strengthen the means of implementation and revitalize the global partnership for sustainable development

Source: https: //sdgs.un.org/2030agenda

sive development. Table 2.1 lists the SDGs published by the UN in 2020, with the pledge that no one will be left behind.

The relations between SDGs and waqf can be conveyed through the discovery of the waqf practices in many aspects. The main goal to eliminate poverty, which is stressed in SDGs, is the focal point to illustrate/portray waqf objectives (Abdullah, 2018). In addition, the Islamic Finance Council UK (2021) reports that the practice of waqf is able to strengthen the commercial Islamic banking and finance sector in achieving the SDGs, developing the education and health sectors, and potentially as alternative financing in socioeconomic activities. For instance, in addressing the vulnerability of the poor and financial stability. Thus, Mohd Zain et al. (2019) affirm that waqf is a valid instrument that can be used in achieving, directly or indirectly, the 17 goals of SDGs.

The participation of the government in realizing the achievement of SDGs cannot be disputed. Hence, in the next section, the discussion deliberates government involvement in waqf practices.

The Participation of Governments to Sustain Waqf Practices

To strengthen the waqf roles in the country, Ismail et al. (2021) stated that waqf should be placed within the scope of the government's involvement in the economy. In Malaysia, the government's involvement in higher education to encourage the use of waqf is of great value, where waqf is seen as one way to sustain educational income.

In other contexts, governments can play their role in various ways by involving the private sector. Ismail et al. (2021) added that participation in the private sector in today's global economy will increase economic efficiency. Innovation in the economy can be better driven when there are many incentives for the private sector to move. In general, the role of waqf institutions can be seen when there is high participation by the private sector through voluntary actions and this can reduce government intervention in the economy.

At the same time, Cizakca also (1998) believes that the waqf program will contribute significantly to a large reduction in government spending. In addition, Cizakca (1998) views that waqf should be given serious attention in providing the most important social services by the government at no cost. However, the Islamic economy has not yet received a large contribution to this waqf, where the practice of waqf is able to gradually eliminate *riba*. In this context, *riba* means usury or interest (World Bank Group, 2016). *Riba* allows a transaction that has the element of interest (Bank Negara Malaysia, 2007). Ahmad et al. (2011) explain that interest by definition is an additional amount paid/received on the principal amount according to an agreement due to a time period attached thereof. The element of interest is strictly prohibited in Islam. In addition, Ambrose et al. (2015) also investigated the role of waqf as an instrument that can reduce government debt. One of the recommendations is that the government needs to spread philanthropy to the community (Ambrose et al., 2015). For example, the economic success of waqf in history must be spread. Specifically, for the Muslim community, the government should spread the benefits of Islamic waqf.

Thus, the government may participate in the waqf through the government's properties (waqf *irshod*) or through collaborations with private companies.

Waqf irshod

Abu Bakar et al. (2020) state that the waqf practices were booming during the time of Al-Ayubiyin's rule in Egypt. The government at that time took the initiative by handing over the government's properties to religious interests, namely waqf *irshod*. The examples of waqf *irshod* were waqf *nablis* used to liberate the Islamic hostages captured by the crusaders in 564H (1168M); 'Said al-Suada House' waqf built for the use of widows and orphans; al-Khibaniah Farm waqf; Khaisariah and al-Shufiah wells waqf in al-Bahnasawiah district; school waqf such as al-Nasirriah al-Shafieh School, al-Qamhiyyahm, al-Malikian in Fayyum and al-Fatimii Palace hospital waqf.

Government appointed institution to manage waqf

The government can appoint private entities to manage waqf assets. As mentioned in The World Bank Group et al. (2019) report, Kuwait and Singapore are examples of nations applying modern waqf management techniques. In South Africa and the United Kingdom, waqf is run by a community-based trust and charitable institutions.

In Kuwait, the Kuwait Awqaf Public Foundation (KAPF) is established as an independent governmental body. KAPF administers all aspects of waqf in Kuwait, including investing and managing the assets, administering the deeds, training waqf personnel, and raising public awareness about waqf. KAPF's main responsibilities include encouraging people to establish new waqf, managing existing waqf, and allocating funds for activities and for the investment of the assets. KAPF coordinates with governmental and non-governmental bodies for the establishment of Shariah-compliant *awqaf* projects to achieve waqf objectives. Waqf funds in Kuwait have independent management teams that contribute to their development with an integrated vision aimed at achieving the community's needs.

In Singapore, The Islamic Religious Council of Singapore (MUIS), under the Administration of Muslim Law Act (AMLA), governs the religious affairs of Muslims in Singapore, including the administration of *zakat*, halal certification, management and administration of waqf, hajj, mosques, and madrasahs. MUIS provides internal guidelines and ISO standards for the appointment of *mutawallis*. These processes include statutory screening for criminal and bankruptcy records. Other criteria include age and educational background. Where there are no private trustees for a particular waqf, MUIS becomes the trustee.

In South Africa, as a non-Muslim country, *zakat* and waqf institutions have been established under the Non-Profit Organization (NPO) Act of 1997. The Act provides an administrative and regulatory framework for NPOs. According to the Act, each NPO must have a constitution that outlines the objectives and the various issues related to the membership and operations of the organization. An NPO must also specify the organizational structures and mechanism for its governance, keep accounting records of its income, expenditure, assets, and liabilities in accordance with generally accepted accounting practices, and must prepare annual financial statements. The Act encourages NPOs to maintain adequate standards of governance, transparency, and accountability. The National Awqaf Foundation of South Africa (Awqaf SA) was established in 2000 as an NPO. This community-based charitable organization is aimed at investing endowment funds for various community development programs.

In the United Kingdom, the Charity Commission (CC) for England and Wales acts as a regulator to register and supervise charities there to ensure that the public can support charities with confidence. The Commission is an independent, non-ministerial government department accountable to Parliament. The Commission is also accountable to the First-tier (Charity) Tribunal and the High Court for the exercise of its quasi-judicial powers. The Commission has five statutory objectives which are to:

a.   increase public trust and confidence in charities;
b.   promote awareness and understanding of the operation of the public benefit requirement;
c.   promote compliance by charity trustees with their legal obligations in exercising control and management of their charities;
d.   promote the effective use of charitable resources; and
e.   enhance the accountability of charities to donors, beneficiaries and the public (The World Bank Group, INCEIF, & ISRA, 2019).

The Commission's Board is responsible for strategic oversight of the Commission. In particular, it is responsible for developing strategies, monitoring progress, overseeing legal matters, providing corporate governance and assurance, and managing corporate risks. It comprises a Chair, two members with legal qualifications, one member with knowledge of the conditions in Wales, and four additional members with relevant skills and expertise in technology, accountancy, risk, security, and the charity sector. The Board is currently supported by five committees.

In conclusion, managing waqf by government can be achieved through a government's properties (waqf *irshod*), collaborations with private companies or government-appointed institutions. Thus, the next section discusses the roles of governments and the UNDP as a UN network body helping, especially developing countries, in implementing waqf.

THE PARTICIPATION OF UNITED NATIONS DEVELOPMENT PROGRAMME IN HELPING IMPROVE THE WAQF EXERCISE TO ACHIEVE SDG

The United Nations Development Programme (UNDP) is the United Nations' (UN's) global development network, advocating change and connecting countries to knowledge, experience, and resources to help people build a better life. UNDP works in about 170 countries helping to eradicate poverty, reduce inequalities and exclusion, and build resilience so countries can sustain progress. UNDP plays a critical role in helping countries achieve the SDGs. UNDP focuses on three areas – sustainable developments, democratic governance and peacebuilding, and climate and disaster resilience. UNDP works in collaboration with governments on development programs and projects (UNDP. org). The importance of highlighting UNDP in the waqf sector is that UNDP works together with individual countries aiming to achieve the identified goals by 2030 (Abduh, 2019).

An example is how the United Nations in Saudi Arabia cooperated with the Kingdom of Saudi Arabia (KSA) in developing and managing waqf. Five SDG agendas are being implemented in Saudi Arabia (United Nations Saudi Arabia, 2021).

1. SDG10 – reduced inequality
KSA prioritizes vulnerable groups consisting of women, disabled persons, and orphans. Two waqf funds are established (partnership with local banks) to collect funds for orphans, *Al-Inma Awqaf* fund and *Ensan* fund. Both funds were established in 2019 and are licensed by the Financial Market Authority and the General Authority for *Awqaf* (GAA) and managed by Alinma Investment Company. KSA established homes for the weak, occupied by elderly men, women, widows, and divorced people. It is free housing facilities, called Rubats (meaning inn, stopping place).

2. SDG4 – quality education
Between 2005 and 2007, Saudi universities pioneered taking advantage of waqf to provide additional income to the direct support provided by the government, while providing the opportunity for society members and university affiliates to contribute.

Another form of a waqf-based educational institution is when the institution is established and funded by a previously existing waqf. For instance, in 1985, Batterjee family members established a waqf for charitable purposes, which funds Doroob, a non-for-profit company investing in educating the elite school students (gifted and creative) to empower them to become leaders of positive change. Then, Effat University was established in 1999 by the waqf-based King Faisal Foundation as the first female-only university in the Kingdom, offering programs that were never available to women.

3. SDG11 – strong and resilient societies
The COVID-19 pandemic in 2020 has made the achievement of SDGs more challenging. KSA, in collaboration with the government and private sectors, and several waqf donors, established a SAR 500 million Community Fund 'Alssondoq Almojtama'y' as a civil society initiative supporting the government's efforts to mitigate the impacts of the COVID-19 pandemic. It aims to support those segments of society most in need and those most affected by the pandemic, including the poor, the disabled, widows, prisoners' families, the elderly, workers in small professions, students, and those in need who are coming to the Kingdom for *umrah* or visits, and others. The fund covers various fields, including relief, social, educational, health awareness, and housing services.

The Ministry of Health of KSA launched the Health Endowment Fund 'AlWaqf *Alshehhi*' initiative to receive and attract financial and in-kind donations from companies, non-profit organizations, businessmen, and individuals to support the government in its fight against the COVID-19 pandemic.

4. SDG 11 – protection of cultural heritage
Some waqf in the KSA are funding activities that are aligned with SDG 11: sustainable cities and communities, particularly targeted to 'protect and safeguard the world's cultural heritage.' Waqf assets support different kinds of charitable work. Saleh Hamza Serafi Foundation was founded in 2009 and made distinguished contributions toward preserving monuments, arts and crafts, and the heritage of Makkah city. For example, it supports Qiblat Aldonya's online platform providing rich information on Makkah's history, monuments, customs and traditions, dialects, and key figures.

5. SDG 2 – sustainable agriculture and food security
As the Saudi population continues to grow, much more effort and innovation are urgently needed to sustainably increase agricultural production and improve the food supply chain. An example of waqf in the KSA is Abdullah Al-Sulaiman Charitable Foundation which supports date palm agricultural research. Every two years, the foundation provides the 'Abdullah Sulaiman International Award for Scientific Innovation in Dates and Palm Trees' to researchers working on the creation of innovative solutions related to dates and palm trees. Another example is Saleh Al-Rajhi Awqaf. Sheikh Saleh bin Abdulaziz Al-Rajhi endowed farms that spread over 5,466 hectares and have nearly 45 types of date palms. In addition to its contributions to various chari-

table and development areas through its profits, the waqf investment strategy is very much aligned with the sustainable development goals through its organic farming and usage of solar energy.

Indonesia

Another UNDP participation is with Indonesia. In Indonesia, UNDP conducted a workshop with the government of Indonesia to enhance waqf development in 2017. Through this workshop, they were targeting five themes based on the SDGs: no poverty (goal 1), good health and well-being (goal 3), quality education (goal 4), affordable and clean energy (goal 7), decent work, and economic growth (goal 8) and industry, innovation and infrastructure (goal 9). According to the United Nations Development Programme (2017), Indonesia translated the SDGs in their national and local development agendas, including the Nawa Cita (Government's nine priority agenda), and the Medium-Term National Development Plan (RPJMN). It should be noted that different approaches to SDGs are applied based on the current status of the countries, e.g. population factor, education level factors, and so on.

Islamiyati et al. (2021) state that the waqf land assets in Indonesia increase every year. For example, in 2016, the waqf land assets reached 4.359 billion m^2 in 435,768 locations. While in 2017, it reached 4.364 billion m^2, and in 2018 it reached 4.4 billion m^2. In 2019, waqf land assets showed 50,200.38 hectares, spread over 372,322 locations. However, to date, most of the waqf land is limited to use as schools, mosques, or public cemeteries. To formulate the best approaches in utilizing waqf as a means to finance the SDGs, UNDP collaborated with Padjadjaran University's SDGs Center to organize a workshop and focus group discussions that would contribute to building the capacity of both institutions to effectively engage in this area. The workshop has brought together key partners in the innovative financing space, including Badan Wakaf Indonesia, Bank Indonesia, The Ministry of Finance, Otoritas Jasa Keuangan, Badan Perencanaan Pembangunan Nasional, New National Committee for Sharia Finance, established under the President, foundations, and other religious organizations.

Therefore, the UNDP contribution is significant to ensure that waqf development can be achieved with collaboration between governments and countries (for example, the KSA and Indonesia).

SDG Programs in the Malaysia Plan

In Malaysia, waqf achievement and development are derived from the Malaysia Plan. To address this, Malaysia supports the SDG program through the Malaysia Plan and waqf, as part of the strategies to develop the National Waqf Plan. Even though the waqf contribution in the 12th Malaysia Plan is still

Table 2.2   SDGs and the 12th Malaysia Plan (Chapter 2)

Selected targets in Chapter 2	The 2030 Agenda
	SDG 8 – Promote sustained, inclusive, and sustainable economic growth, full and productive employment and decent work for all
Financial services blueprint	SDG 9 – Build resilient infrastructure, promote inclusive and sustainable industrialization, and foster innovation
Capital market masterplan	SDG 16 – Promote peaceful and inclusive societies for sustainable development, provide access to justice for all and build effective, accountable and inclusive institutions at all levels
	SDG 17 – Strengthen the means of implementation and revitalize the global partnership for sustainable development

ongoing, certain sectors have achieved the SDGs target. This section presents waqf contributions and development in six of the chapters in the 12th Malaysia Plan.

Chapter 2 of the 12th Malaysia Plan restores the growth momentum. In this chapter, Malaysia wants to promote Islamic finance (including waqf practices) to achieve SDGs 8, 9, 16, and 17. Malaysia is aiming to offer new services in financial services and the capital market. To achieve the SDG agendas, the social finance instruments (waqf, *sadaqah*, and *zakat*) are aiming to provide financing to low-income communities, broadening Islamic capital market products and services to further support social finance activities (such as waqf), and encourage Higher Education Institutions (HEIs) to explore alternative financing, including waqf and crowdfunding in ensuring the sustainability of the institutions. Table 2.2 summarizes the details highlighted in Chapter 2 of the 12th Malaysia Plan.

Chapter 3 of the 12th Malaysia Plan is propelling the growth of strategic and high-impact industries as well as Micro, Small, and Medium Enterprises. This chapter focuses on high-impact industries in regenerating economic growth. The waqf contributions are shown in halal industries. In 2020, the halal industries successfully achieved SDGs 8 and 9 as high impact industries. During the Eleventh Malaysia Plan, initiatives were undertaken to ensure integrated and comprehensive development of the domestic halal industry. Efforts were focused on the development of halal standards and certification, branding and promotion as well as commercialization of halal products and services. Table 2.3 summarizes the details highlighted in Chapter 3 of the 12th Malaysia Plan.

In Chapter 4 of the 12th Malaysia Plan, waqf implementation is addressed to fulfill SDG 3 and SDG 9 through (i) Improvement in Healthcare Service Delivery, and (ii) Enhancement of Public Affordable Houses Governance since in the 11th Malaysia Plan.

Table 2.3   SDGs and the 12th Malaysia Plan (Chapter 3)

Selected target in Chapter 3	The 2030 Agenda
Halal industries	SDG 8 – Promote sustained, inclusive, and sustainable economic growth, full and productive employment and decent work for all
	SDG 9 – Build resilient infrastructure, promote inclusive and sustainable industrialization, and foster innovation

Healthcare service delivery is enhanced to increase the health status of the rakyat, including the provision of a sustainable healthcare system as well as financial support, improving health literacy among the population, and greater collaboration among stakeholders. The implementation of these initiatives has enabled the rakyat to have better access to quality and affordable services. Thus, waqf implementation elaborates on the provision of financial support and enhancement of public affordable houses governance.

Provision of Financial Support
The *Skim Peduli Kesihatan Untuk Kumpulan B40* (PeKa B40) was launched to address the healthcare needs of the B40 group, focusing on non-communicable disease (NCDs). This scheme offers four benefits, namely health screening, medical equipment, transport subsidy, and incentives to complete cancer treatments. As of the end of 2019, a total of 201,497 individuals or 25 per cent of the target group were registered and screened for NCDs. Meanwhile, contributions were received from various Civil Society Organizations (CSOs), the corporate sector, and the community to enhance healthcare capacity and capability during the COVID-19 pandemic. Multinational companies and other firms also contributed in the form of medical equipment, medicines, reagents, disposable items, and other medical necessities besides donating cash to several COVID-19 funds. The plan also initiated the establishment of Tabung *Wakaf* Kesihatan Negara which focuses on the development of waqf properties and products.

Enhancement of Public Affordable Houses Governance
Measures were undertaken to strengthen the governance of public affordable housing programs. The *Perbadanan PR1MA Malaysia, Syarikat Perumahan Negara Berhad* and *Program Perumahan Penjawat Awam Malaysia (*PPAM*)* were centralized under the Ministry of Housing and Local Government (KPKT) for better governance and coordination. In addition, the *Sistem Bank Data Perumahan Negara* was developed in 2018 to enable data sharing among agencies at the federal and state levels. Public affordable houses were also constructed on waqf land through strategic partnerships among various agen-

Table 2.4   *SDGs and the 12th Malaysia Plan (Chapter 4)*

Selected targets in Chapter 4	The 2030 Agenda
Improvement in Healthcare Service Delivery	SDG 3 – Ensure healthy lives and promote well-being for all at all ages
Enhancement of Public Affordable Houses Governance	SDG 9 – Build resilient infrastructure, promote inclusive and sustainable industrialization and foster innovation

Table 2.5   *SDGs and the 12th Malaysia Plan (Chapter 5)*

Selected targets in Chapter 5	The 2030 Agenda
Income equality through improving monthly income	SDG 1 – End poverty in all its forms everywhere
	SDG 2 – End hunger, achieve food security and improved nutrition, and promote sustainable agriculture
	SDG 3 – Ensure healthy lives and promote well-being for all at all ages
The needs of the female labor force	SDG 4 – Ensure inclusive and equitable quality education and promote lifelong learning opportunities for all
	SDG 5 – Achieve gender equality and empower all women and girls
	SDG 10 – Reduce inequality within and among countries
Youth participation	SDG 11 – Make cities and human settlements inclusive, safe, resilient and sustainable

cies at Federal and state levels with the private sector. A total of 2,934 public affordable houses were developed on waqf land under this initiative. Table 2.4 summarizes the details highlighted in Chapter 4 of the 12th Malaysia Plan.

Chapter 5 of the 12th Malaysia Plan addresses poverty and Malaysia's socio-economic development. Since the Second Malaysia Plan, reducing hardcore poverty and improving the well-being of all Malaysians irrespective of gender, ethnicity, socio-economic status and location have been priorities in Malaysia's development planning. In the 11th Plan, equitable opportunities were provided to enable the rakyat to participate and benefit from economic growth and development. Inclusive development initiatives included raising the income and purchasing power of B40 households (B40), enhancing the capacity of the Bumiputera Economic Community (BEC), empowering minority groups, and addressing inequalities. Table 2.5 summarizes the details highlighted in Chapter 5 of the 12th Malaysia Plan.

In the past five years, the standard of living has improved, as is evident from the increase in median monthly income, better access to healthcare services as well as improvement of basic infrastructure and amenities. However, there are still issues and challenges that need to be addressed in achieving inclusivity for all. One of the challenges is the development of Malay Reserve Land (MRL)

Table 2.6   SDGs and the 12th Malaysia Plan (Chapter 10)

Selected targets in Chapter 5	The 2030 Agenda
Enhancing access to quality education and training	SDG 4 – Ensure inclusive and equitable quality education and promote lifelong learning opportunities for all
Fostering greater industry–academia linkages	
Reforming the labor market	SDG 8 – Promote sustained, inclusive and sustainable economic growth, full and productive employment, and decent work for all

and waqf land is still limited due to a lack of financial capabilities and governance issues. This will be the focus of the 12th Malaysia Plan for the years 2021 to 2025.

Chapter 10 of the 12th Malaysia Plan focuses on developing future talents. Human capital is a key driver of economic growth and socio-economic development. During the 11th Plan, the development of human capital focused on four areas, namely improving the quality of education, transforming technical and vocational education and training (TVET), strengthening lifelong learning (LLL), and increasing the efficiency of the labor market to meet industry demand. Efforts to accelerate human capital development succeeded in increasing school enrolment and TVET intake as well as improving the quality of universities and labor productivity. The quality education delivered by the various learning institutions remains a priority for Malaysia as it forms the foundation for building a resilient economy. A high-quality education system will produce a high-caliber talent pool that possesses relevant industrial skills and is highly adaptable. However, there are still issues that persist in the labor market and in the education system that need to be addressed. These issues include low compensation of employees (CE), inefficient labor market, limited access to quality education, and weaknesses in the governance of educational institutions. The COVID-19 pandemic has caused a spike in the unemployment rate and new norms in the way people work and businesses operate. This necessitates the realignment of the labor market as well as the education and training landscape. In line with job market demand, waqf instruments could be developed and fulfill the SDG programs, as explained in Table 2.6.

Chapter 11 of the 12th Malaysia Plan focuses on boosting digitalization and advanced technology.

The advancement of technology and the ever-changing global economy have highlighted the urgency for the nation to adopt a more agile and proactive approach in moving towards a high technology-based economy. The Fourth Industrial Revolution (4IR) through the intensification of digitalization and the emergence of new technologies is affecting human life in unprecedented ways. In the 11th Plan, measures were undertaken to accelerate innovation and tech-

Table 2.7   SDGs and the 12th Malaysia Plan (Chapter 11)

Selected targets in Chapter 11	The 2030 Agenda
Accelerating innovation and technology adoption	SDG 9 – Build resilient infrastructure, promote inclusive and sustainable industrialization and foster innovation
Providing quality infrastructure	
Advancing digital economy	
Accelerating research, development, commercialization and innovation	

nology adoption as well as provide quality infrastructure to support economic growth. However, the challenges remain in embracing digitalization such as lack of digital infrastructure, fragmented governance, insufficient capacity, and capability as well as unaffordability to access digital services. These challenges have led to the slow growth of the digital economy and widened the digital divide. Low technology adoption, insufficient investment in research, development, commercialization, and innovation (R&D&C&I) as well as lack of talents have affected progress in modernizing the economy. The emergence of disruptive technologies also needs to be managed to harness the economic potential while safeguarding the interest of the rakyat.

In the 11th Malaysia Plan, there was no specific focus on the waqf development. Generally, the 11th Malaysia Plan mentioned accelerating innovation and technology adoption and providing quality infrastructure to fulfill SDG 9. In the meantime, the 12th Malaysia Plan targets advancing the digital economy, accelerating research, development, commercialization, and innovation to achieve SDG 9. This could be the opportunity for the government (policymaker) and corporate firms to collaborate in working on the waqf models in SMEs to arrive at all the plans in the 11th and 12th Malaysia Plans. Table 2.7 summarizes the details.

Hence, from the Malaysia Plan, waqf instruments have placed the roles in the main sectors, namely in financial sector, SME sector (halal industry), healthcare and infrastructure for socio-economic development, labor sector and digitalization and the technology sector. In the meantime, a study from Abu Bakar et al. (2020) shows that waqf played a significant role in achieving SDGs in Malaysia.

Abu Bakar et al. (2020) claim that waqf could be one of the most important elements in achieving SDGs. Concerning the importance of sustainable development in Islam, Abu Bakar et al. (2020) state that *maqasid shariah* is a very important approach as a discipline that can be applied to the existing SDGs. In the context of *Shariah*, the Kuwait Finance House (n.d.) states that Shaykh Muhammad Al-Tahir Ibn Ashur defined *Maqasid* of the Islamic law as the objectives or purposes behind the Islamic rulings. He explained the knowledge of *Maqasid al-Shari'ah* is important for mujtahids to not only understand or interpret the texts of Shariah but also to derive solutions to contemporary problems faced by Muslims. The concept of *Maqasid Shariah* provides clear guidance and framework to the process of *ijtihad* in solving the issues conforming to the human interest while complying with the will of God. Kuwait Finance House (n.d.) explains that *Maqasid Shariah* is divided into three according to the 'levels of necessity', these three categories are necessities (*daruriyat*), needs (*hajiyat*) and luxuries (*tahsiniyat*). Here, waqf activities and practices are under Necessity. Kuwait Finance House (n.d.) clarifies that necessities are essential elements for human beings. The absence of these elements may cause harm and damage to human life. Examples of necessities are shelter, food, and clothes. The necessities are further classified by the scholars into five elements of preservations. The objective of Islamic rulings is mainly to protect these five elements from any harm. These preservations are known as:

- Protection of Faith or religion (*din*)
- Protection of Life (*nafs*)
- Protection of Lineage (*nasl*)
- Protection of Intellect (*'aql*)
- Protection of Property (*mal*)

To simplify, Abu Bakar et al. (2020) state that, in the waqf context, every activity, project, and development of the waqf undertaken should be evaluated following the requirements of the *Shariah*. Further explanation and relation of necessities (based on *Maqasid Shariah*) and relation with SDG are shown in Table 2.8.

To understand the concept, Abu Bakar et al. (2020) explain the five *maqasid shariah* classification that contributes to SDGs, as shown in Table 2.8. These are (i) protection of faith (hifz al-din); (ii) protection of life (hifz al-nafs); (iii) protection of human progeny (hifz al-nasl); (iv) protection of intellect (hifz al-aql), and (v) protection of wealth (hifz al-mal).

The protection of faith (hifz al-din) focuses on reducing vulnerabilities, which in turn is believed to help strengthen their faith. Protection of life (hifz al-nafs) aligns with Islamic Finance in ensuring healthy lives and promoting well-being for sustainable development.

The protection of human progeny (hifz al-nasl) aligns with Islamic finance that helps people escape the poverty trap, promotes peace and protection of the environment. Healthy nourishment, quality education, and making children more productive in the future are in line with the protection of intellect (hifz al-aql).

Lastly, the protection of wealth (hifz al-mal) promotes wealth which can help generate economic activity (SDG 8) and a social safety net (SDGs 1 and 3).

Table 2.8   *SDGs and the classifications based on* maqasid shariah

SDG Goals	Maqasid shariah
SDG 1: End poverty in all forms everywhere.	Protection of Intellect (Hifz al-'aql)
	Protection of Faith (Hifz al-din)
	Protection of Wealth (Hifz al-mal)
SDG 2: Zero hunger. End hunger, achieve food security and improve nutrition and promote sustainable agriculture.	Protection of Intellect (Hifz al-'aql)
	Protection of Faith (Hifz al-'aql)
	Protection of Life (Hifz al-nafs)
SDG 3: Good health and well-being. Ensure healthy lives and promote well-being for all ages.	Protection of Intellect (Hifz al-'aql)
	Protection of Faith (Hifz al-'aql)
	Protection of Life (Hifz al-nafs)
	Protection of Progeny (Hifz al-nasl)
	Protection of Wealth (Hifz al-mal)
SDG 4: Quality education. Ensure inclusive and equitable quality education and promote lifelong learning opportunities for all.	Protection of Intellect (Hifz al-'aql)
SDG 5: Gender equality. Achieve gender equality and empower all women and girls.	Protection of Life (Hifz al-,,nafs)
	Protection of Progeny (Hifz al-nasl)
SDG 6: Clean water and sanitation. Ensure availability and sustainable management of water and sanitation for all.	Protection of Faith (Hifz al-'aql)
	Protection of Life (Hifz al-nafs)
SDG 7: Affordable and clean energy. Ensure access to affordable, reliable, sustainable and modern energy for all.	Protection of Progeny (Hifz al-nasl)
SDG 8: Decent work and economic growth. Promote sustained, inclusive and sustainable economic growth, full and productive employment and decent work for all.	Protection of Life (Hifz al-,,nafs)
	Protection of Wealth (Hifz al-mal)
SDG 9: Industry, innovation and infrastructure. Build resilient infrastructure, promote inclusive and sustainable industrialization and foster innovation.	Protection of Intellect (Hifz al-'aql)
SDG 10: Reduced inequalities. Reduce income inequality within and among countries.	Protection of Faith (Hifz al-'aql)
	Protection of Wealth (Hifz al-mal)
SDG 11: Sustainable cities and communities. Make cities and human settlements inclusive, safe, resilient and sustainable.	Protection of Life (Hifz al-,,nafs)
	Protection of Progeny (Hifz al-nasl)
SDG 12: Responsible consumption and production. Ensure sustainable consumption and production patterns.	Protection of Progeny (Hifz al-nasl)

SDG Goals	Maqasid shariah
SDG 13: Climate action. Take urgent action to combat climate change and its impacts by regulating emissions and promoting developments in renewable energy.	NA
SDG 14: Life below water. Conserve and sustainably use the oceans, seas and marine resources for sustainable development.	NA
SDG 15: Life on land. Protect, restore and promote sustainable use of terrestrial ecosystems, sustainably manage forests, combat desertification, and halt and reverse land degradation and halt biodiversity loss.	NA
SDG 16: Peace, justice and strong institutions. Promote peaceful and inclusive societies for sustainable development, provide access to justice for all and build effective, accountable and inclusive institutions at all levels.	NA
SDG 17: Partnerships for the goals. Strengthen the means of implementation and revitalize the global partnership for sustainable development.	NA

Source: Abu Bakar et al. (2020)

Here, Abu Bakar et al. (2020) affirm that SDGs are evolving in societal well-being and are in line with *maqasid shariah*. The waqf contribution plays a significant role in achieving the SDGs by 2030.

As waqf institutions play important roles in supporting the SDG strategies, the next section will explain the contributions of waqf through the connection between Islamic Social Finance and the SDGs.

THE ISLAMIC SOCIAL FINANCE AND THE SUSTAINABLE DEVELOPMENT GOALS

The connection between Islamic Social Finance (ISF) and SDGs is aligned with bringing balance to the physical, emotional, mental, and spiritual needs of the community in supporting overall economic growth (Mahadi et al., 2021). To highlight on the matter, a report by the Islamic Finance Council UK (2021) mentions that ISF supports sustainable development via Goals 1, 2, 3, and 4.

As SDGs 1, 2, and 3 aim to achieve no poverty, zero hunger, and good health, Islamic Finance Council UK (2021) highlights that the integration of waqf and *zakat* with the financial sector can play a major role in realizing these SDGs. In pursuing the SDGs in socio-economic activities, philanthropic instruments such as waqf, *zakat*, and sadaqah will rank supreme due to their potential in instilling cooperation, solidarity, and alternative finance. Many scholars mentioned that waqf and *zakat* funds are among the main pillars that should be examined as dominant factors of an Islamic financial instrument, especially in eradicating hunger and poverty. In addition, unlocking the potential of Islamic finance by introducing innovative products such as waqf, *zakat*, and Islamic microfinance could improve financial inclusion, financial sector stability, and, ultimately, enhance the contributions of Islamic finance to the SDGs.

Waqf is considered an important Islamic instrument and can directly be used for poverty alleviation and financing other SDGs, mainly the education and healthcare sectors. This was established over 1,400 years ago, whereby ISF such as *zakat*, waqf, and *sadaqah* made a great impact in poverty alleviation and the enhancement of social and economic development, including education, health care, and infrastructure development.

Goal 4 refers to quality education. This goal stresses equitable quality education opportunities for all with no discrimination. In this regard, most participants agreed that Islamic law emphasizes the importance of seeking knowledge, as the Messenger of Allah (pbuh) said, 'Seeking knowledge is an obligation upon every Muslim (man or woman)' (Sunan Ibn Mājah, 224). Many scholars mentioned that Islam has enacted many ways to spread knowledge and fight ignorance, such as charities and *zakat*, as well as waqf, which is used to develop education (Educational Endowment).

Thus, ISF has a bright potential to support efforts towards an inclusive economy and to accomplish the SDGs. The next section will explain how ISF, as a third-sector economy, plays its role especially in waqf instruments.

The Roles of Waqf as a Third-sector Economy

Islamic Social Finance (ISF) is known as the third sector of the economy (The World Bank Group et al., 2019). The World Bank Group, INCEIF, & ISRA (2019) identified ISF instruments, such as *zakat* and waqf, as capable of addressing the humanitarian crises in the Muslim world.

The third sector is voluntarism or the voluntary sector, where the primary objective is not for profit, but rather to defend and safeguard the welfare of society. The term third sector is used to refer to a variety of organizational types, including charities, non-government organizations, self-help groups, social enterprises, networks and clubs, volunteer groups, cooperatives, and social movements (Mohd Arshad & Mohamed Haneef, 2016). In other words, the third sector is unique and its effectiveness is closely related to the number of volunteers. The greater the public involvement in volunteer activities, the greater the role of the third sector in building and enhancing a country's socio-economic status. This sector usually involves voluntary activities such as the provision of social services, environmental protection and conservation, education, and various other activities that are often overlooked by the public and private sectors. In other words, the third sector acts as a pool of funds for financing small and mega projects, for example, waqf hospital, waqf education, and waqf smart city. Therefore it makes waqf part of the nation's way of life (Najim, 2021).

The redistribution of wealth to others is crucial for it is proven in helping the stabilization of a country's economy. Waqf has a solid connection to shariah principles. The former Malaysian Minister of Religious Affairs, Mohamad Al-Bakri (2020), quotes waqf as the 'Economic system of the people, led by the people, for the people. It leads to the creation of the third sector that complements the public and private sectors'. Thus, it is recognized that waqf is in the third sector of economy. This section highlights the roles of waqf in the third-sector economy from the societal and economic perspectives.

Society

Waqf institutions also play a major role in ensuring a fair distribution of the economy's wealth and income. Ismail (2021) stated that waqf could positively impact the redistribution of wealth through the wealthy's voluntary contributions for the public purpose.

This kind of voluntary solution has a much better result than tax allocation and government transfer spending, as the tax instrument involves a greater cost for its execution. The cost of collecting taxes will create unnecessary burdens for the government due to a lack of proper tax formulation. It also includes a great cost in the transition of government spending. In contrast, the collection costs will be very low in the form of waqf and, in most cases, it will entail no expense whatsoever. It will also help in empowering the vulnerable people and the poor in society for greater economic prosperity. It will assist in ensuring the financial inclusion of small-scale businesses.

This will help boost their financial capacity. In order to maximize the potential role of cash waqf, a standard institution needs to be established with proper legislative backings. Islamic teachings highly recommend that people, in addition to *zakat*, give alms to the poor or spend money for the benefit of the public through the waqf system. Through such a cooperative process, people help the authorities strengthen society's situation. As waqf created by rich people helps society in general and the poor, this function aims to mitigate the impact of disparity in income and wealth. Unlike the short-term effect of government fiscal policies, the waqf institution may remove society's propensity to concentrate on wealth.

Poverty and inequality of wealth have always been among the most important and enduring problems faced by societies. There are ways to deal with the issues of deprivation, beginning with preventive measures. An effective way to alleviate poverty, as Sadeq (2002) considered, is a charity, which plays a role and could potentially be a successful way of overcoming these acute problems (Van Slyke and Newman, 2006). The charity has many forms, but one that has the characteristic of perpetuity is a long-term form of charity. The institution of waqf in the Islamic system is such a perpetual charity.

It is possible to create and maintain long-term assets that produce income flows through waqf. These assets support the production process and the creation of wealth. Waqf may play an essential role in alleviating poverty by concentrating primarily on the vulnerable as major beneficiaries of their benefits. Waqf can also be designed to disseminate awareness and coaching skills in the creation of entrepreneurship among the poor because microfinance alone cannot create wealth unless combined with entrepreneurial skills. Indeed, all technical assistance programs can be grouped as waqf, including poverty alleviation (Obaidullah and Khan, 2008).

As a potential financial instrument, waqf has played an essential role in resolving the social problems of society (*ummah*). For example, for the problems of Mahammadiyah waqf land in Magelang, Indonesia it was observed that empowerment of the land was not optimized due to lack of financial resources, unproductivity, and the presence of incompetent and professional Nazhirs. The solution to these problems is through collaboration with financial institutions in collecting cash equivalents, land specifications, formulating a special legal framework for empowering Muhammadiyah waqf, and training for the development of the capacity of the areas (Medias et al., 2019).

Economy

The economic development in Islam is seen as a multi-dimensional activity and a process of integrating human and social development. In other words, the economy and material development in Islam must be placed under the broader scope of human development. It relates to the comprehensive character that is inseparable from the moral, spiritual, and material aspects, the improvement of human well-being, and it achieves human well-being through the progress, reorganization, and reorientation of the entire economic and social system, and through spiritual upliftment, in accordance with Islamic teachings. The index is based on economic growth, justice in the distribution of income and wealth, and a healthy social environment that is in line with Islamic norms and values (Abu Bakar et al., 2020).

Cizakca (1998) claimed that waqf could achieve a better income distribution in the economy, which is one of the modern economic goals. In this process, a secondary role is certainly assigned to taxation. There are other implications: a lower tax burden means a rise in consumers' and producers' surpluses and a reduction in the 'dead-weight tax cost.' Therefore, lower taxes would positively affect gross output while reducing costs at the same time. Consumer prices would, therefore, decline and prevent inflationary growth.

Budiman (2014) mentions that well-managed waqf properties would generally improve the country's economic development. During the Ottoman Empire, waqf and the economy were highly connected in a positive direction. The economy of the country was also progressing as the waqf institution flourished. The greater the size of waqf properties, the greater the size of the private sector's participation, and the greater the economic progress. There is a positive correlation between the private sector's active participation in the economy and national economic growth. More interestingly, as the waqf offers public goods and thus sufficiently fulfills society's needs, it solves the problem of the under-supply of public goods. Ku Hanani (2021) mentioned that waqf can help in controlling unsustainable debts, for waqf to finance public expenditures or at least part of it.

Giving waqf as a part of spending in the way of God also stimulates the circulation of wealth in society, as envisaged by the Holy Qur'an (al-Hashr [59]:7). The Prophet's inspiration to do waqf and the eternal rewards for life and the afterlife motivated Muslims to do this noble charity. This intervention could help stop the economy's hoarding and idle capital that prevents it from stagnating and being active, eventually leading to economic progress.

Thus, waqf is believed to have two economic approaches that can enhance long-term investment. First, the ability of the property to invest, and the second is to use the property from the proceeds. Both of these properties have proven that devotional practices are not only an act of worship promised by God with great rewards but at the same time play an important role as an investment mechanism for generating long-term funding sources.

This chapter wraps up the roles of waqf as sustainable economic development. Each subtopic highlights the SDGs as the main connection. First, this chapter describes the SDGs in the 2030 Agenda where contents were more on how waqf practices could be blended in the SDG activities. In addition, with UNDP's participation, the SDG aims can be achieved consistently. Second, the participation of the government to sustain waqf practices was also described. It is explained that managing waqf by the government can be applied through government properties waqf *irshod*, collaboration with private companies or government appointed institutions to manage waqf. Third, the roles of the government and UNDP in assisting waqf activities in developing countries to achieve the SDGs plan. The KSA presents how waqf has improved in their country and how Indonesia actively collaborates with UNDP to develop waqf practices. Then, this topic also addressed Malaysia's supports for the SDG programs through the Malaysia Plan and waqf as part of the strategies to develop the National Waqf Plan. Even though the waqf contribution in the 12th Malaysia Plan is still ongoing, there are certain sectors that have achieved the

SDG targets. This chapter also shared waqf contributions and development in six chapters in the 12th Malaysia Plan. Next, this chapter also summarized the contribution of waqf through the connection between ISF and SDGs.

Finally, this topic explains waqf as a third-sector economy. Waqf is a form of charity with special features that has permanence and continuity. The waqf concept can enhance long-term investment. The third sector is voluntarism or the voluntary sector where the primary objective is not for profit, but rather to defend and safeguard the welfare of the society. This third sector is unique, and its effectiveness is closely related to the number of volunteers. The greater the public involvement in voluntary activities, the greater the role of the third sector in building and enhancing a country's socioeconomic status. This sector usually involves voluntary activities such as the provision of social services, environmental protection and conservation, education, and various other activities that are often overlooked by the public and private sectors.

The next chapter will explain how waqf contributes to sectors.

3. Waqf contributions to sectors

This chapter focuses on the role of waqf contributions in selected sectors: (i) education, (ii) real estate, (iii) agriculture, (iv) tourism, (v) Islamic Social Institutions, (vi) health industry, (vii) Real Estate Investment Trust (REIT), and (viii) Financial technology (Fintech). These selected sectors are among the largest contributors to waqf activities. Most of the contributions in this sector are in the form of contemporary waqf (such as cash waqf, waqf assets, sukuk, waqf shares, etc.). The importance of highlighting these sectors is to show that waqf activities can be implemented in various ways and aspects. It is proven that the purpose and activities of waqf are not only for religious purposes, such as building mosques and cemeteries but for social development. Therefore, with the increasing understanding of the scope of waqf, this chapter shares studies to show the various roles of waqf.

WAQF EDUCATION

Historically, waqf in education is the second-largest waqf contribution after waqf for mosques. Waqf in education has been implemented since the time of the Prophet Muhammad (pbuh) when he built the Quba mosque in Medina, which was not only a place of worship. Although religious education is usually covered by waqf on mosques, education, in general, has been the second-largest recipient of waqf revenues (Ahmad & Hasan, 2018).

Since the beginning of Islam, the growth of waqf education was reported in the early seventh century. Education has been financed by waqf as well as other voluntary contributions, such as the *awqaf* of the Ayubites (1171–1249) and the Mamalik (1249–1517) in Palestine and Egypt. Moreover, Jerusalem had 64 schools at the beginning of the twentieth century, all of them were waqf and supported by waqf properties in Palestine, Turkey, and Syria. Of these schools, 40 were made waqf by Ayubites and Mamalik rulers and governors (Hasan & Ahmad, 2017).

Rusydiana et al. (2021) reviewed the relationship between waqf on education and other waqf plans, Sustainable Development Goals (SDGs), civilization's history, and the government responsibilities. The sustainability character of waqf makes the plans essential to the SDGs, particularly the fourth aim. In the golden time of Islam, an evolved civilization had quality and great education based on social funds, notably waqf, followed by European countries with an endowment fund. Therefore, it was stated that waqf may be a remedy for financing issues.

Since then, the waqf contribution in education has evolved in many aspects. Two examples are given: cash waqf and the use of waqf in higher education.

Cash Waqf

Abdel Mohsin (2013) reported that Kuwait has succeeded in establishing an International Islamic Charitable Organization (IICO) to provide humanitarian aid worldwide through a cash waqf scheme in the educational sector. This scheme succeeded in financing educational and social charitable services, such as sponsoring orphans, providing medical care, financing the teaching of Arabic and Islamic subjects, and paying the salaries of teachers in Chad, Gambia, the Philippines, Albania, and Kosovo.

In Malaysia, Islamic Finance Council UK (2021) reported that Bank Muamalat Malaysia Berhad (BMMB) introduced a cash waqf scheme which is used to develop education, health care, infrastructure and to train young entrepreneurs. Plus, the proceeds from the Sukuk Ihsan issuance, which is exclusively targeted at institutional investors, were channeled to Yayasan AMIR, a not-for-profit organization to improve the accessibility of quality education in Malaysian government schools. It has reached over 65,000 students and 83 trust schools across ten states in Malaysia.

Hussin (2021) examined the guidelines for waqf employment in Higher Education Institutions (HEIs) as shown in the University Transformation Programme (UniTP) Purple Book as well as the Guidelines for Management of Waqf in Education Institutions Book. This study used a qualitative research technique that included a semi-structured interview and a theological approach to analyze state enactments and previous studies to gain a comprehensive knowledge of the issue under consideration. The study concluded that the Malaysian government is highly concerned about the legitimacy of waqf creation in its HEIs. Although the parameters given appear to be generic, they provide stakeholders with a starting point for establishing waqf in their organizations. Hussin et al. (2021) discussed the notion of good governance in HEIs through extensive literature reviews and content analysis, as well as how the concept may be applied to the management of waqf in HEIs. The findings indicated that good governance procedures are acknowledged as a critical success element for the long-term viability of waqf in HEIs. The future development of waqf for HEIs will be heavily reliant on effective administration. Good governance procedures can inspire faith in interested parties or waqf to commit their endowments to the mutawalli.

Meanwhile, Ayuba et al. (2020) determined the types of waqf education available in Sekolah Agama Rakyat (SAR), with an emphasis on the state of

Kedah, Malaysia, and examined how waqf education is regulated and maintained to provide long-term benefits. The study carried out in-depth interviews and document analysis with two SARs management in Kedah. It was found that several waqf educations exist in SARs, namely cash waqf, al-Quran waqf, lands, buildings and furniture waqf. The SAR administrator is responsible for the management of this education waqf and must guarantee that the current education waqf assets may be utilized in a more effective manner in order to generate constant and ever-growing benefits.

In Indonesia, Saidon et al. (2019) illustrated waqf in education, practiced in Pondok Modern Darussalam Gontor (PMDSG). A successful waqf-oriented educational institution in Indonesia was used to demonstrate waqf in education in Indonesia (PMDSG). The study adopted both primary and secondary data to look into the administration of the PMDSG, specifically its waqf management. The philosophy practiced is to accept any donation or sponsorship from any agency, but it is not obligated by the conditions of the donor. This PMDSG administration delivers services that are autonomous, transparent, and trustworthy. According to the findings of the study, the waqf-based education model used in PMDSG is a viable method to be used in today's educational system.

In conclusion, waqf plays an important role in education. Waqf in education has been implemented since the time of the Prophet Muhammad (pbuh). Two examples are given: cash waqf and the use of waqf in higher education. Cash waqf finances the educational and social charitable services, such as sponsoring orphans, providing medical care, and financing the teaching. Waqf in higher education indicates that good governance procedures are a significant critical success element for the long-term viability of waqf in HEIs.

WAQF PROPERTIES

Properties are one of the waqf assets. Omar et al. (2013) conclude the terms of waqf assets (based on *fuqaha* terms) include the characteristics of physical (*'ayn*), usufruct, and power of rights ownership. They mention that an asset must have two basic criteria; first, it must be affordable and tradable, and it can be either tangible or intangible. If the goods do not have value due to insufficient amounts such as a grain of rice or drop of water, then they cannot be categorized as an asset. Second, the goods must have beneficial usage at all times (not during an emergency only). If the goods are beneficial among only a few people but do not have value from Syariah's standpoint, such as liquor or pork, then they also cannot be classified as valuable. Omar et al. (2013) also explained that property is also defined as any asset extracted from the earth in the form of food, plantation, and livestock. Similarly, as mentioned in Chapter

1, the administration and management of waqf assets must adhere to the principles stipulated in Islam as follows.

Al-Wāqif

Al-Wāqif refers to an individual who gives the asset he owns to be used as waqf on Allah's path. Several criteria have been outlined to the *al-wāqif*. The *al-wāqif* must fulfill several conditions, such as sound mind, independence (not a slave), maturity, and not being naïve.

Al-Mawqūf Bih

Assets to be used for waqf must be something that is beneficial and has value in Islam and is owned by the *al-wāqif*. In addition, the assets must also be known and stated in detail to the waqf trustee. Waqf assets can be divided into two main categories. The first category is fixed waqf assets (ghayru al-manqūl) such as land or building. The second category is non-fixed waqf assets (al-manqūl) such as mashaf, cash, and other items deemed valuable from an Islamic perspective.

Waqf Beneficiary (*Al-Mawqūf 'Alayh*)

Waqf beneficiaries comprise individuals and also groups such as institutions and associations. Waqf trustees can also channel the waqf assets' benefits to help non-Muslims under the '*kafir zimmi*' category, who obey the Muslim ruler. If this non-Muslim group retaliates against the ruler, the waqf assets' benefits are forbidden to be distributed to them because they have changed to become *kafir harbi*.

Şīghah Waqf (Ijāb & Qabūl)

Waqf asset's offer, and acceptance declaration, comprises *ijāb* and *qabūl* which can be made in writing or orally. The term *Şīghah* is everything that refers to the mutual consent between both parties who are dealing in the waqf arrangement. *Şīghah* declaration is very important, and it is considered necessary to explain to the community and family members with regards to the status of the waqf assets.

Thus, it can simplify the meaning of waqf properties as a fixed waqf asset (ghayru al-manqūl) or non-fixed waqf asset (al-manqūl). This section discusses the examples of waqf on the development of waqf properties in construction of roads, buildings, Sukuk in waqf assets, and waqf shares in real estate investment trusts (REITs).

The first example is the construction of roads. Abu Bakar et al. (2020) mention that Princess Siti Zubaidah, the wife of Caliph Harun al-Rashid, built the road from Baghdad to Mecca from her waqf properties. She built the water canal as she realized that the pilgrims had difficulties and hardships to get a water supply while visiting Mecca and Medina. This water canal is known as the Canal of Ain Zubaidah and is an underground canal that runs through the desert hundreds of miles from Baghdad to the holy city of Mecca. The canal was built in the 808M by applying technology that was beyond human thought at the time. Interestingly, all the funding and maintenance costs for building the canal were fully utilized by her waqf resources and money.

The second example is in developing a building. Omar et al. (2018) mention that Tabung Haji (TH) and Majlis Agama Islam Wilayah Persekutuan (MAIWP) collaborate in developing and managing the Bank Islam Tower. According to the agreement, TH financed the cost of construction and, upon completion, its subsidiary TH Properties manages the assets. Since its completion, the property has been leased to Bank Islam and is called Menara Bank Islam (Bank Islam Tower). The role of MAIWP is to provide the land as a waqf institution. TH acts as the developer and manager of the property.

The third example is the waqf development involving the issuance of sukuk, which is not entirely new to the market. There have been successful Sukuk issuances for the development of waqf assets in several jurisdictions (for instance, Singapore and Saudi Arabia). These issuances demonstrate how Sukuk, being a Shariah-compliant capital market instrument, can be innovatively structured to support the financing for the development and redevelopment of waqf assets into viable income-generating properties.

The Securities Commission Malaysia (2014) mentions Sukuk as waqf assets in Saudi Arabia. Sukuk al-Intifa'a for the development of Zamzam Tower, Makkah. In Saudi Arabia, the issuance of Sukuk al-intifa'a (timeshare) has been successfully implemented to develop one of the apartment towers near the Grand Mosque in Makkah. In this transaction, a construction and real estate company, Munshaat Real Estate Projects Co. (Munshaat) was awarded a 24-year lease to construct one of the seven towers (Zamzam Tower) on the land adjacent to the Grand Mosque, which is owned by the King Abdul Aziz waqf for the Two Holy Mosques (The Waqf).

In this transaction, the developer, Munshaat was granted the lease over the waqf land. The Sukuk issuance was to finance the construction cost of said tower. This was achieved via a forward lease contract (*ijarah mawsufah fi dhimmah*). Under the forward lease, Munshaat leased the asset under construction to the Sukuk holders (for 22 years) who paid the lease rental in advance in one lump sum.

Due to restrictions on ownership of non-Saudis of real property rights in Makkah, the Sukuk holders would enjoy the usufruct of the assets after its construction based on time-sharing slots. The time-sharing rights under the forward lease were evidenced by the issuance of *sukuk al-intifa'a*. The advance lease rental (Sukuk proceeds) was used by Munshaat to pay for the 24-year lease rental on the waqf, and the construction costs of Zamzam Tower.

The interesting part of sukuk al-intifa'a is the recognition of a new asset class upon which the Sukuk is based. This new asset class is in the category of usufruct (*manfa'ah*). More specifically, it involves the right to benefit or enjoyment (*haq al-intifa'a*) in the form of time-sharing in the use of common property. This Sukuk is fully negotiable. It can be sold, leased, lent, given, bequeathed, exchanged, and delayed (subject to certain conditions). The investor participates by purchasing the Sukuk and paying the value in advance, plus payment of annual charges for maintenance and managerial service.

The fourth example is waqf shares in real estate investment trusts (REITs). These are collective investment schemes (typically in the form of trust funds) that pool money from investors to buy, manage and sell real estate. The type of real estate that REIT invests in includes residential or commercial buildings, retail or industrial lots, or other real estate-related assets, such as shares in listed or unlisted securities of property companies. The objective is to obtain returns on investment generated from rental income plus any capital appreciation that comes from holding the real estate assets over an investment period. Unitholders receive their returns in the form of dividends or distributions and capital gains during the holding period (Securities Commission Malaysia 2014).

In general, the well-managed waqf properties would enhance economic progress in the country.

Ibrahim and Ibrahim (2013) remind us that it had been attested in the past, particularly during the Ottoman Empire, that waqf and economy were highly connected in a positive direction. As the waqf institution was flourishing, the country's economy was also advancing. The bigger the size of waqf properties, the bigger the size of private sector involvement, and the more progress the economy made. There is a positive correlation between the active private sector's participation in the economy with national economic progress. More interestingly, since the waqf provides public goods and thus fulfills society's needs adequately, it solves the problem of undersupply of public goods, so often observed in conventional economies. Given the wide involvement of the private sector, the provision of waqf for public purposes is so abundant and even creates an excess supply of public goods rather than their scarcity in the Islamic economy (Cizakca, 1998).

WAQF AGRICULTURE

The agriculture sector is one of the most powerful industries and has the potential to end extreme poverty and feed around 9.7 billion people by 2050. The growth in this industry is two to four times more effective in increasing incomes among the underprivileged population (Azganin et al., 2021). An alternative viable financing solution is required to enable small farmers to access funds, end poverty and address several other problems such as food security and hunger. In this sense, one of the main philanthropic concepts practiced throughout Muslim history is waqf, which has contributed tremendously towards addressing economic and social issues in various sectors, including agriculture.

Thus, the importance and benefits of waqf agriculture, issues in agriculture related to land, and effort in waqf agriculture through a crowdfunding scheme are discussed. Azganin et al. (2021) list three important benefits of waqf agriculture.

First, the large proportion of the cultivated areas of waqf lands in different countries. Turkey itself has one-third of its cultivated area being waqf lands.

Second, the investment of waqf properties through different financing modes could generate good returns for society.

Third, rather than depending on banking facilities, which seems to be the only flagship of the economy to introduce specific financing services for farmers, the establishment of a waqf trust could be considered a possible alternative instrument to activate idle agricultural lands.

Normally, despite the lack of capital, farming and agriculture operators are still reluctant to involve banks in meeting financing needs (Bilal Khan et al., 2021). In fact, farmers prefer informal financing, such as landlords and families, rather than financing their agricultural plans through banks. Such funding alternatives are driven by farmers' way to eliminate the complicated bureaucracies of banks and their high interest rates. The waqf fund will be used to provide credit to farmers, which will help them to grow and produce a better yield.

Another issue is about certain countries experiencing very bad situations by having fewer agricultural lands, food insecurity, malnutrition of the people, especially children, and famine at the same time (Abduh, 2019). When agriculture is not sustained, there will be threats to the food security agenda of the country. Issues in the food security of a country can trigger many unwanted situations, including malnutrition of the younger generation. Severe food insecurity could result in famine and eventually a non-conducive political situation to run the country. In the worst scenario, food insecurity issues could trigger a civil war. Therefore, issues on sustainable agriculture and food security are very important to discuss.

Efforts being made in the agriculture sector are through cash waqf and crowdfunding methods. According to Abduh (2019), the Islamic Social Finance (ISF) of waqf al-awāriḍ is one of the solutions. The research laboratory can be based in one country within the region and member countries of the region can arrange for waqf funds from their people with a special purpose to build a research laboratory and fund its research activities for the benefit of societies within the region.

Abdel Mohsin (2013) mentions that Kuwait has successfully managed to establish an International Islamic Charitable Organization (IICO) to provide humanitarian aid worldwide through a cash waqf scheme: farms and productive projects. This scheme succeeded in funding different farms and agriculture projects in the Philippines, Bangladesh, India, and Uganda.

In crowdfunding, Azganin et al. (2021) mention that several studies found that crowdfunding platforms can address liquidity issues, specifically in the waqf. For example, Agropay is a crowdfunding project which creates opportunities for all agribusiness actors who interact on a single platform. This platform provides specific functions for investors who can select from a wide range of agricultural projects accessible via smartphones, while the investment is made online. This platform creates competitiveness between suppliers and increases price competition, which further improves the sustainability of agriculture products.

Another example is the waqf crowdfunding platform named "Hasanah Crowdfunding Model" in Indonesia. The Wakaf Hasanah project has played a vital role in financing and developing various waqf projects in Indonesia. Fifty-three waqf projects have been financed through this platform, with a total fund of more than three billion rupiahs. According to this platform, the parties involved are the project manager (*Naẓir*), waqf founders, and the platform operator.

Therefore, the potential of investing in waqf lands has largely enabled waqf authorities to generate significant returns in the agriculture sector. Hence, this enables waqf institutions to provide end beneficiaries with the required services and needs.

WAQF TOURISM

The first aspect to be discussed in this section is the role of waqf activities in developing the tourism industry. Accommodation, historical, and shopping centers are part of the waqf tourism that has been developed. Then, the importance and benefits of waqf and the potential of waqf in tourism are clarified.

The role of waqf can be seen through the services of accommodation centers in mosques and hotels that have the potential to grow in the tourism industry. Abdul Razak (2019) states that mosques have a history, heritage, and aesthetic value that can attract domestic and foreign tourists to visit. The mosque has its value as a tourist attraction. Che Man et al. (2019) also mentioned tourism activities related to the mosque's location and accommodations, as many mosques are located along the travel route. They highlight that a *Musafir* home (rest house for travelers) could add value to tourism activities. For instance, two mosques in Malaysia, Sultanah Bahiyah Mosque, Kedah, and Perlis Osmaniah Mosque, have been used to generate waqf funds. Besides the concept of a *Musafir* home for charity, the accommodation in the mosque's area helps travelers who have difficulty finding any places to sleep at a rea-sonable price. Moreover, the *Musafir* home in Osmaniah mosque in Perlis was established to fulfill places to sleep for travelers as they discovered the difficulty of finding places to rest as this place is near the tourist shopping area attraction at Padang Besar, Perlis.

In Malaysia, examples of four hotels built on waqf land are as follows: (i) Melaka (Puteri Bay Hotel, formerly known as Pantai Puteri Hotel), (ii) Perak (Sri Warisan Hotel), (iii) Terengganu (Grand Puteri Hotel), and (iv) Negeri Sembilan (Klana Beach Resort). Many parties are involved in developing these hotels. First, the State Islamic Religious Council (SIRC), the owner of waqf land, which is looking for suitable land to build hotels. Next, the government provides capital to build hotels, and JAWHAR, as the project manager, ensures that such accommodation must comply with a Shariah-compliant tourism industry. The hotel will become the SIRC's property, which will later be handed over to Yayasan Wakaf Malaysia (YWM) to be managed for at least 20 years. YWM will lease the hotel companies that are interested in operating it. This rental income will generate waqf funds and be returned to SIRC by YWM. The result of the generation of waqf funds guarantees the continuity of operation of shariah-compliant hotels (Che Man et al., 2019).

These hotels must fulfill the requirements of shariah-compliance. In shariah-compliance practices, the hotels must provide prayer mats, the Quran, and Qibla direction indicators, not sell or serve alcohol, and not allow unmar-ried couples to stay. In terms of operations, shariah-compliant hotels serve halal food and beverages, have Islamic design, room layouts, prayers-friendly facilities, business transactions using Islamic banking, the appearance of employees who cover their awrah, conducive treatment, and environment (Mohd Noor et al., 2019). Islam views tourism as a form of appreciation and thinking in seeking the blessings of Allah SWT. Therefore the consumption of alcohol, prostitution, promiscuity between men and women, gambling, and other similar activities while traveling are prohibited in Islam. What is impor-tant is the implementation of the main basic concepts of shariah that need to be emphasized by shariah-compliant hotel operators. In short, it involves *halal* and *haram* matters (Mohd Noor et al., 2019).

The exciting thing about the hotel concept of shariah-compliance is that hotels have become a preference among Muslim tourists, which excites Muslim tourists to travel more – the demand for hotels with Muslim concepts is capable of boosting the economy of countries. To support this, Hassan et al. (2021) mention that, according to the World Travel and Tourism Council, the tourism sector is worth about \$245 billion of the GDP of the Middle East Countries, and it provided 6.7 million jobs before COVID-19 impacted the economies, resulting in a decline in GDP per capita income.

Besides hotels, Che Man et al. (2019) mention that the waqf mechanism can also serve to build and preserve historical places. The next part will present the examples of preserved historical places. The welfare complex of Sultan Haskei Jerussalam, founded in 1552 by the wife of Caliph Sulaiman of the Uthmaniyyah government in Palestine and Lebanon, was financed through a waqf fund. This waqf mechanism also plays a dynamic role in the restoration of the entire area of abandoned and damaged buildings and the replacement of the old and obsolete with new buildings. Moreover, in Egypt, *waqif* plays a role as the developer in developing the regions that were dilapidated and destroyed. They will buy the buildings and develop the area through the construction of new buildings.

In another context, the waqf fund can also be used to develop historical areas which become tourist attractions, or recreational areas that have the potential to be developed as a focal point. For example, creating an Islamic-themed park in strategic locations through the waqf fund obtained from the surrounding communities. Responsible developers can build and develop the theme parks by offering waqf shares to the public who are keen to join in developing the theme park. Through the construction of the Islamic theme park, it will indirectly attract tourists thus this can improve the economy of local communities.

Che Man et al. (2019) also mention the construction of shopping centers based on waqf, which are associated with tourism activities as there are many tourist attractions that focus on shopping. For example, Pulau Langkawi – which is known as the duty-free island in Malaysia; as well as the states of Kelantan, Terengganu, Sabah, and Sarawak in Malaysia. These areas are often filled with tourists who like to do recreational activities while shopping. Given this situation, the authorities and individuals can work together to develop waqf land in potential areas by building a complex or a shopping center that meets the needs of the community and tourists. Sultan Al-Mansour Qalawun of Egypt had used waqf funds to build a complex in 1285 consisting of a hospital, madrasah, *sabil kuttab* (public drinking place), and his tomb.

Furthermore, an income-based property is also built around the complex, such as shops, warehouses, homes as well as agricultural lands. Revenues earned from waqf properties are used to fund various economic activities, which provide a return of one million dirhams per year. This proves that developed waqf properties can bring a substantial revenue and change the socio-economic landscape of the local community.

Therefore, it is confirmed that waqf can be operated and managed in tourism activities. It is important to know how to manage the fund, whether the waqf fund is obtained from cash waqf or waqf land, so the countries can boost the economy. The benefits of developing waqf tourism are urging Muslims to travel, not only for social activities but also to strengthen the relationship among Muslim countries and expand the economy.

WAQF IN ISLAMIC FINANCIAL INSTITUTIONS

This section focuses on the waqf products and services (for example, *musharakah* and *qard al-hasan*) in Islamic financial institutions. The discussion focuses on the importance and benefits of waqf in Islamic financial institutions, the potentials of waqf, and what efforts have been made. Most of the examples are based on the waqf in Islamic financial institutions practiced in Malaysia.

Principally, the relation of waqf in Islamic finance institutions refers to the roles and functions of waqf, which is described as charity profit-making organizations. According to Gabil et al. (2020), the institutions may appear as privately-owned financial institutions, social banking institutions, income-generating institutions, and institutions interested in charity activities and the redistribution of wealth. This section will discuss both 'Islamic window' and fully-fledged institutions that offer waqf as their products and services.

'Islamic window' refers to services based on Islamic principles provided by a conventional bank. Some commercial banks offer Islamic banking services through dedicated windows or sections. A 'fully-fledged institution' refers to those Islamic banks that operate using Islamic principles entirely.

In 2021, there are over 1500 Islamic financial institutions (fully-fledged) worldwide across 80 countries (Bank Negara Malaysia, 2022). Six Islamic banks in Malaysia are involved in the implementation of waqf. They are Affin Islamic Bank Berhad, Bank Islam Malaysia Berhad, Bank Muamalat Malaysia Berhad, Bank Rakyat, Maybank Islamic Berhad, and RHB Islamic Malaysia Berhad. For waqf schemes, six cash waqf schemes are offered in Islamic financial institutions: waqf shares scheme, deposited cash waqf scheme, compulsory cash waqf scheme, corporate waqf scheme, deposit product waqf scheme, and co-operative waqf scheme (Abdel Mohsin, 2013).

Table 3.1   The establishment of ten cash waqf schemes

Cash waqf schemes	Descriptions
Water wells scheme	This scheme succeeded in constructing dams, digging surface wells and supplying the poor and needy with watercoolers in India, Jordan, Somalia, Africa, Bangladesh, Nigeria and Somalia
Educational scheme	This scheme succeeded in financing educational and social charitable services such as sponsoring orphans, providing medical care, financing the teaching of Arabic and Islamic subjects and paying the salaries of teachers in Chad, Gambia, the Philippines, Albania, and Kosovo
Mosques scheme	This scheme succeeded in building and maintaining many mosques in many countries, such as Egypt, Kazakhstan, China, and Togo
Health care scheme	This scheme succeeded in providing medical equipment and building hospitals in Egypt, building dental clinics in Palestine, building hospitals in the Philippines, and IICO hospitals for cancer patient care in Kuwait
Training centers scheme	This scheme succeeded in funding many centers, such as computer training centers in Africa, training institutes in Indonesia, Nigeria, and Uganda
Farms and productive projects	This scheme succeeded in funding different farms and agriculture projects in the Philippines, Bangladesh, India, and Uganda
Orphans scheme	This scheme succeeded in sponsoring orphans, building and maintaining orphanages and providing orphans with proper education in Uganda
Seasonal projects	This scheme succeeded in financing the cost of preparing meals for breaking the fast/iftar during the month of Ramadhan, and distributing the meat during the month of sacrifices in Malawi, Nigeria, Cambodia, Kurdistan, and Somalia

Cash Waqf Schemes

According to The World Bank Group et al. (2019), there are currently 15 Islamic banks registered as official Islamic Financial Institution Recipients of Cash Waqf (IFI-RCW) in 2019. In Malaysia, the Islamic banks that promote and practice cash waqf include Bank Muamalat Malaysia Berhad (BMMB), which introduced the cash waqf scheme in collaboration with Perbadanan Wakaf Selangor (PWS, Selangor Waqf Corporation). Abdel Mohsin (2013) mentions that Kuwait has succeeded in establishing an International Islamic Charitable Organization (IICO) to provide humanitarian aid worldwide. Table 3.1 shows the establishment of ten cash waqf schemes through IICO.

   Abdel Mohsin (2013) reported that the UK NGO institutions play an important role in the Muslim community. One of these institutions is Islamic Relief. It was established in 1984 as an international relief and development charity organization. Under this scheme, the waqf scheme was established as a Waqf Future Fund (WFF). The main objective of this WFF is for various long-term projects provided in many countries, such as education waqf schemes, water, and sanitation waqf schemes, orphans waqf schemes, Qurbani waqf schemes, healthcare waqf schemes, emergency and relief waqf schemes, and income generation waqf schemes. Many countries have benefited from these schemes such as Indonesia, Kosovo, Palestine, Albania, Sudan, Afghanistan, Bosnia, Mali, Bangladesh, Pakistan, India, China, Kosovo, Egypt, Iraq, South Africa, Niger, and Kenya.

Deposit Cash Waqf Schemes

Cash waqf scheme deposits are a public waqf. Abdel Mohsin (2013) mentions that cash waqf deposit schemes have been practiced in Singapore, Bahrain, and South Africa. The flow of how to deposit cash waqf, or in some terms called direct cash waqf, operated according to these steps:

(1) The founder contributes directly to a specified religious authority or a specified institution by depositing money as cash waqf to a specific bank account.
(2) The bank then invests the money according to the agreement with the religious authority or the specified institution.
(3) The religious authority or the specified institution as the trustee will receive the revenue generated after investment and then distribute it to the said charitable areas.

However, Abdel Mohsin (2013) clarifies that it is difficult to trace how the banks invested the accumulated cash waqf scheme before channeling it to the beneficiaries.

In Singapore, deposit cash waqf was created in the twentieth century. At that time Muslimin Trust Fund Association and other Muslim businesses and individuals endowed cash to be invested as cash waqf. The main purpose of this investment is to finance the burials of poor Muslims, give aid to Muslim orphans, give aid to the Alsagoff School, and finance other charity projects (Abdel Mohsin, 2013).

While, in South Africa, the deposit cash waqf was created to encourage contributors to contribute to the National Awqaf Foundation (AWQAF SA) cash waqf fund. The collected cash waqf was invested in a portfolio of income-generating instruments. Revenue is then spent on programs ranging from providing funding for skills development, tree planting, and education projects to financing religious institutions.

Meanwhile, in Bahrain in 2006, the Central Bank of Bahrain, such as the Bahrain Monetary Agency (BMA), together with several Islamic financial institutions, established deposit cash waqf. The objectives are to finance the development and implementation of Islamic finance training programs under the Bahrain Institute of Banking and Finance (BIBF). The investment returns succeeded in financing the public awareness programs and research and publication programs.

Waqf Sukuk

Another initiative in developing *awqaf* is to connect waqf with securitization. In line with this endeavor, the International Shariah Research Academy (ISRA) for Islamic Finance is currently working together with the IsDB on issuing waqf sukuk worth US$100 million. The funds will be used to set up and operationalize sheep and dairy farms and renewable energy projects in selected jurisdictions. The income generated will benefit *awqaf* beneficiaries and will be used for charitable and social purposes all over the world. This is considered an innovative project both from the economic and Shariah perspectives.

In Singapore, sukuk *musharakah* was introduced for developing commercial buildings on waqf land. Sukuk *musharakah* was also used for the development of an old mosque in Bencoolen Street, Singapore. This initiative was spearheaded by Warees Pte Ltd (Warees), a subsidiary of the Islamic Religious Council of Singapore or Islamic Religious Council of Singapore (MUIS).

Between 2001 and 2002, Warees successfully developed two pieces of waqf lands in Singapore through the issuances of sukuk musharakah in which US$60 million was raised. One of these projects was the redevelopment of an old mosque into a multi-storey complex comprising a modern mosque, a three-storey commercial building, and a full-service 12-storey apartment block with 84 units in Bencoolen Street in 2002. The financing of the project was done through the issuance of S$35 million sukuk *musharakah*. The *musharakah* was a joint venture among three parties, i.e. MUIS (*baitulmal*), Warees, and MUIS (Waqf). The sukuk was fully subscribed by institutional investors. The structures of this sukuk issuance about the redevelopment are in the form of partnerships and distribution of return (Securities Commission Malaysia, 2014).

In Saudi Arabia, the issuance of sukuk *al-intifa'a* (timeshare) has been successfully implemented to develop one of the apartment towers near the Grand Mosque in Makkah. In this transaction, a construction and real estate company, Munshaat Real Estate Projects Co. (Munshaat) was awarded a 24-year lease to construct one of the seven towers (Zamzam Tower) on the land adjacent to the Grand Mosque, which is owned by the King Abdul Aziz Waqf for the Two Holy Mosques (The Waqf). In this transaction, the developer, Munshaat was granted the lease over the waqf land. The sukuk issuance was to finance the construction cost of the said tower. This was achieved via a forward lease contract (*ijarah mawsufah fi dhimmah*). Under the forward lease, Munshaat leased the asset under construction to the sukuk holders (for 22 years) who paid the lease rental in advance in one lump sum. Due to restrictions on ownership by non-Saudis of real property rights in Makkah, the sukuk holders would enjoy the usufruct of the assets after its construction based on time-sharing slots. The time-sharing rights under the forward lease were evidenced by the issuance of sukuk *al-intifa'a*. The advance lease rental (sukuk proceeds) was used by Munshaat to pay for the 24-year lease rental on the waqf, and the construction costs of Zamzam Tower.

Waqf Shares

This scheme is a public waqf that emerged in the last decades in Muslim-majority countries, such as Malaysia, Indonesia, Kuwait, and also the UK. The main objective of this scheme is to generate money or to raise funds from the public to support the welfare of society. The collection of this kind of funds is meant to finance lawful goods and services needed in the different societies (Abdel Mohsin, 2013). Waqf shares have been issued by Kuwait Awqaf Public Foundation (KAPF), Islamic Relief Waqf in the United Kingdom, and Perbadanan Wakaf Selangor in Malaysia.

In the Islamic Relief Waqf in the United Kingdom, the dividends arising from the investing activities of the waqf institution that is tasked with managing the shares become the benefit to be distributed to the needy and destitute. The benefits of these waqf shares would be for global distribution, wherever a need may arise. Since the designated beneficiaries are assigned through the waqf deed, there is no restriction to spend locally before considering global needs, as in the case of *zakat*. Islamic Relief in the UK has applied the purchase of waqf shares by donors for many of the projects and initiatives they manage such as an education waqf scheme, water and sanitation waqf scheme, orphans waqf scheme, and others.

Waqf could be linked with sukuk (Islamic bond), and it can be used to support products such as agriculture and fisheries. This type of sukuk could be issued by using waqf land as the underlying asset where the land would be used productively to generate profits. For example, waqf land could be leased to SMEs at attractive rates, and the revenues generated plowed back into those SMEs to support their growth or used to support the Sustainable Development Goals more broadly.

Among the initiatives implemented by Malaysia is strengthening its waqf development. In 2017, the Chairman of the Securities Commission, Datuk Syed Zaid Albar, affirmed that Malaysia has launched the world's first waqf initial public offering (IPO) (Securities Commission Malaysia, 2019). The World Bank Group et al. (2019) state that waqf-based shares have been issued under the social enterprise model whereby the money received from the Initial Public Offering (IPO) will be channeled to improve the Larkin Sentral bus terminal in Malaysia. After buying the shares, the shareholders can donate their shares to the trustee and manager of the waqf so the dividends can be used to support the deprived class of society and single-mother families. Opportunities are also being provided to small business owners to open shops at the terminal at discounted rental rates.

This initiative can be viewed as consistent with the UN's SDG 10: reducing inequality (The World Bank Group, INCEIF, & ISRA, 2019). Waqaf Saham Larkin Sentral property Berhad (Larkin Sentral) is an initiative implemented by Waqaf An-Nur Corporation Berhad (WANCorp) for the welfare and economic interests of the ummah as a whole.

Therefore, it is understood that Islamic financial (refers to banking) institutions offer six types of waqf scheme: waqf shares scheme, deposited cash waqf scheme, compulsory cash waqf scheme, corporate waqf scheme, deposit product waqf scheme, and co-operative waqf scheme offered by Islamic financial institutions.

WAQF IN THE HEALTH INDUSTRY

In general, the health industry is related to healthcare including hospitals and clinics. This subtopic emphasizes waqf services in hospitals. A waqf hospital refers to a hospital that provides free treatments while providing other needs to the community. It is created to provide facilities for the community especially for the less fortunate and the poor. Its existence in the Islamic world has a positive impact primarily on the welfare of the people. Historically, waqf hospitals began around the eleventh century, which showed an advancement in the system of birmaristan (Persian or Dar Al Shifaa in Arabic and Darussyifa in Turkish) or hospitals. The word *Bimaristan* originates from Persian and has the same meaning as hospital. *Bimar* in Persian means disease and *stan* is location or place or place of disease. In this subtopic, the history of waqf and how waqf contributes and evolves in the health industry are discussed.

The concept of a waqf hospital, which was established at the commencement of the Islamic empire, bears all the treatment costs, medicines, beds, mattresses, remuneration, and wages of medical officers and nurses, and pharmacies and takes care of the maintenance of related buildings. There is no special treatment for patients regardless of their race, religion, and gender. One of the first waqf hospitals was Fatih Hospital, built in Istanbul, the administrative center of the 'Uthmaniyyah'. The operation of waqf funds for Fatih Hospital was started in the fifteenth century.

A study by Rozali and Alias (2019) states that Fatih Hospital received waqf funds from Sultan Mehmet II's waqf institution. Through this waqf fund, various hospital activities could be systematically carried out, including the daily wage payment of doctors, nurses, and staff at Fatih Hospital. Recreational equipment and musicians were provided to help patients. At that time, the hospital did not only treat patients but also furnished training facilities for medical trainees. It is said that the Islamic hospital was the world's pioneer hospital to keep all patients' records and medical reports. However, the hospital stopped operating in the mid-nineteenth century due to certain factors, such as an earthquake that destroyed most of the hospital buildings.

Interestingly, the history shows that Nabawi Mosque in Madinah was the first mosque to provide medical treatments in its courtyard. It was said that Caliph Al-Walid opened the first hospital in Damsyik with medical equipment and expertise. In AD 1246, the first waqf hospital, Al-Qawarun Hospital, was established and treated 8,000 patients every day for free. This hospital was built and operated according to the concept and practice of waqf.

Other waqf hospitals around the world through the centuries include the following. Shishli Children Hospital in Istanbul was founded by a health waqf in 1997. The hospital and mobile medical rescue groups who traveled from village to village were managed through the properties and assets of the waqf. In Yemen, there was already an outstanding waqf hospital called Mata Hospital. In Indonesia, Cempaka Putih Hospital is a waqf hospital that has been operating for a long time. Patients are given free treatment while trainee medical officers are also not burdened by any tuition fees. In Malaysia, Universiti Sains Islam Malaysia (USIM) is the only public HEI that operates a waqf-based health center. Malaysia also has the An-Nur Clinic which operates using the concept of waqf. It is reported that Penawar Hospital Group and KPJ have been involved with waqf hospitals for a long time and have about RM500 million in hospital waqf funds.

Waqf An-Nur in Malaysia is another example that can be emulated by others. It provides healthcare and dialysis services to the less fortunate in Malaysia, both Muslims and non-Muslims alike. Vehbi Koç Foundation (Vehbi Koç Vakfı) in Turkey is perhaps the first documented case of a corporate waqf. Second, strengthening the collaborations among sectors (*zakat*, waqf, and *sadaqah*) in enhancing synergies and outcomes in social initiatives. For example, through mobilizing clinics, a joint venture among Bank Muamalat and Wakaf Selangor and two hospitals (vehicles being transformed into mobile clinics) and targeted to services in the disaster area that require medical and health attention.

Abdel Mohsin (2013) mentions that Kuwait has managed to establish an International Islamic Charitable Organization (IICO) to provide humanitarian aids worldwide through a cash waqf scheme: a health care scheme. This scheme has succeeded in providing medical equipment and building hospitals in Egypt, building a dental clinic in Palestine, building a hospital in the Philippines, and IICO hospital for cancer patient care in Kuwait.

Therefore, it is understood that waqf contributes to many aspects in the health industry. The history of the waqf concept starts with being responsible for all the treatment costs, medicines, beds, mattresses, remuneration, and wages of medical officers and nurses, pharmacies, and also taking care of the maintenance of related buildings. Plus, there is no special treatment for patients; regardless of race and religion, each patient is treated until recovered. Female and male patients are assigned doctors of the same gender.

WAQF IN REAL ESTATE INVESTMENT TRUST (REIT)

In this subtopic, the establishment of the Awqaf Properties Investment Fund (APIF) by The Islamic Development Bank (IsDB) in 2001 will be discussed. APIF finances the development of waqf real estate properties, with a special focus on the properties to be invested for the utilization of their income as per the condition(s) of the endower, since this form of waqf would be conducive to repaying the financing from the income of the property itself. As a fund that distributes dividends, APIF brings an element of impact investment to encourage resource mobilization for waqf. APIF uses leasing and *istisna'* for construction of residential buildings, office/commercial buildings, and mixed-use development of waqf lands. The resources of APIF come from IsDB along with other organizations, comprising Ministries of *Awqaf*, *Awqaf* Organizations, nonprofit organizations, Islamic banks, and individual investors.

APIF is financing the Waqf income-generating commercial and residential real estate properties. It does not finance the construction of schools, universities, mosques, health facilities, and the like. As of the end of 2020, the APIF portfolio shows 55 completed or active projects, totaling US$1.22 billion in value. APIF helps waqf and charitable organizations fulfill their mandate by providing required resources to develop waqf land owned by these organizations, renovate waqf properties, and/or purchase property to be utilized as waqf. Supported waqf institutions or charitable organizations are then expected to utilize the rental income generated by such projects to support their social and charitable activities.

WAQF IN FINANCIAL TECHNOLOGY (FINTECH)

The evolution of technology has now transformed the business environment into a more dynamic one. The Islamic finance industry is certainly no exception to the technological revolution that challenges today's Islamic financial practice norms. The integration of these technologies, when explored to the optimum, can provide the solution to the socio-economic issues underlying the problem of access to basic services. Thus, the evolution of financial technology or Fintech opens the opportunity for waqf instruments to contribute.

The CEO of Architect defines Islamic Fintech as is an adjustment of financial, technological developments to Islamic finance and ethical finance (Dinar Standard, 2021). Wan Ismail (2020) states that the emergence of new information technology in the financial services industry is known as "Fintech". In this subtopic of Fintech, the importance and benefits of waqf in Fintech, issues, and effort in waqf Fintech are discussed.

The importance of technology advancement has benefited the waqf channel. Quoting the keynote address by His Royal Highness Sultan of Perak Sultan Nazrin Muizzuddin Shah,

> Technological advances are being made every day, and emerging breakthroughs in fields, such as artificial intelligence (AI), robotics, the Internet of Things (IoT), nanotechnology, and biotechnology will, no doubt, further enhance the potential of the waqf system in ways that we cannot imagine today.

Even the Ministry of Economic Affairs (2018) recommends emerging technologies such as AI, big data analytics (BDA), financial technology (Fintech), and IoT for waqf.

According to a research firm called Venture Scanner, Fintech companies are categorized into 13 groups by their businesses: lending, personal finance, payments, equity financing, remittances, retail investing, institutional investing, security, infrastructure, business tools, crowdfunding, online banking, and research and data. This implies the need to look at the concrete forms of financial services among various types when talking about the actual transactions (Dinar Standard, 2021). The following section discusses the waqf platforms, services and also waqf development made by the country.

To date, the implementation of waqf Fintech is still at the initial stage. Yoshida (2019) studied how Fintech or financial services could be enhanced by the high utilization of information and communication technologies (ICT), which can enable the potential capability of cash waqf. Yoshida named it "Fintech-enabled cash waqf". Fintech-enabled cash waqf here is one of the basic forms of Fintech, which is generally called "crowdfunding". Crowdfunding acts as a platform on the internet that provides information on each project for the sake of potential investors. If an individual decides to invest a certain amount of money in the project he/she would like to support, he/she does so by clicking a relevant button on the website or the application software. The funds are provided typically in four ways: donation; reward (physical products such as manufactured goods); loan; and equity. For a collection of funds from the public, Fintech can play a huge role with extremely high efficiency of acquiring information and payment from the viewpoint of the potential provider of funds. A potential donor (*waqif*) of cash waqf will go to the website of the Waqf World and provide details of the waqf amount and the *waqif* him/ herself. The collected funds will be invested into real estate and equities.

Another approach of waqf Fintech is blockchain, a distributed public ledger that records transactions. It is a technology that has recently begun to make a major impact on the financial system. It is predicted that its role and applications will continue to increase in the future. Integrating blockchain with waqf could go a long way to addressing the problems of transparency and trust that currently hamper broad-based public participation in waqf. Blockchain is still a developing technology; however, according to The World Bank Group et al. (2019), there are Shariah issues that need to be resolved before applying it to waqf.

In Malaysia, Abu Bakar et al. (2020) mention that 93 Fintech companies are offering Islamic financial services including social finance solutions. Banking and financial institution structure, and innovative financing for waqf are introduced to replace traditional modes of finance.

In Singapore, there is a company named Finterra that offers a system that uses blockchain technology, called Waqf Chain. It not only speeds up the process of raising waqf funds for the development of a waqf project but also ensures transparency in its management.

In Indonesia, the potential for QR-code based digital payments has been explored to stimulate financial inclusion efforts across all segments (Deloitte Indonesia, 2021). This initiative is a synergy of joint ventures among the Indonesian government, financial institutions, and even Fintech companies. Another platform is a peer-to-peer (P2P) crowdfunding platform, which presents several promising opportunities for the development of cash waqf programs. Currently, P2P crowdfunding platforms are already widely used in Southeast Asia, including in major Muslim markets such as Indonesia and Malaysia (Deloitte Indonesia, 2021).

With innovations such as Fintech and digital payments, collection and reporting flows may be faster and more efficient. This innovation motivates many waqf programs and can prevent non-existent waqf projects from happening if they are not closely supervised. There are several cases of fraud against traditional cash waqf practices. Proper accountability may not be present if it is not controlled or monitored. With that, this Fintech service can offer technology integration for more comprehensive and efficient access and as one of the channels in the waqf chain.

The cash waqf which is currently operating based on a physical waqf certificate may be transformed to the waqf-digital certificate.

In conclusion, Fintech may be able to provide a significant solution. Conceptually, the use of ICT will make redistribution of income from the rich to the lower-income group in a much more efficient manner, because it can enhance cash waqf, social investments, microfinance, and other types of social finance. Of course, the efficiency for the rich to fund opportunities and project details is essential. In accelerating the integration of this technology into the creation of solutions based on Islamic financial instruments, the role of scholars must be strengthened in enhancing the mastery of technology so that these pioneering solutions can achieve the desired sustainability goals. Thus, the integration of technology in the implementation of social financial instruments can not only ensure a more efficient and orderly execution but also contribute to strengthening Islamic finance in the future.

Notably, it is imperative to highlight the waqf roles in different sectors to understand that waqf can contribute to any method/source. In this chapter, the main sectors that waqf contributes to – education, properties, agriculture, tourism, Islamic Social Institution, health industry, Real Estate Investment Trust (REIT), and financial technology (Fintech) – have been discussed. In education, this chapter discusses cash waqf and the use of waqf in higher education. Cash waqf finances educational and social charitable services, such as sponsoring orphans, providing medical care, and financing the teaching. Waqf in higher education indicates that good governance procedures are acknowledged as a critical success element for the long-term viability of waqf in HEIs. For properties, this chapter is divided into two categories: fixed waqf asset (*ghayru al-manqūl*) or non-fixed waqf asset (*al-manqūl*). In this category, the example of waqf is focused on the development of waqf properties in the land (real estate) or buildings (school, hospital, bridge, and road) and Sukuk in waqf assets. In general, well-managed waqf properties would enhance the country's economic progress. Since the waqf provides public goods and thus fulfills society's needs adequately, it solves the problem of undersupply of public goods.

The growth in the agriculture industry is two to four times more effective in increasing incomes among the underprivileged population. The potential of investing in waqf lands has largely enabled waqf authorities to generate significant returns in the agriculture sector. Hence, this enables waqf institutions to provide end beneficiaries with the required services and needs. On the other hand, the role of waqf in developing the tourism industry can be seen in several aspects namely accommodation centers, the historical center, and shopping centers. The waqf in tourism plays an important role in urging Muslims to travel, not only for social activities but also to strengthen the relationship among Muslim countries and expand the economy. Thus, it is timely to consider tourism as preserving the historical buildings and shopping centers in tourism activities in waqf locations as part of the attraction to revitalize the economy of the country.

Islamic financial institutions relate to the institutions of waqf which are described as charity profit-making organizations. This section focuses on the waqf products and services (for example, *musharakah* and *Qard-al-Hasan*) in Islamic financial institutions. It includes the discussion of the importance and benefits of waqf, the potential of waqf in Islamic financial institutions, and what efforts have been made. For the health industry, the discussion refers to the waqf services in hospitals. Waqf hospital refers to a hospital that provides free treatments while providing other needs to the community. It is created to provide facilities for the community, especially for the less fortunate and the poor. Its existence in the Islamic world has a positive impact, primarily on the welfare of the people, thus it is understood that waqf contributes to many aspects of the health industry.

The history of the waqf concept starts with being responsible for all the treatment costs, medicines, beds, mattresses, remuneration, and the wages of medical officers and nurses, pharmacies, and also taking care of the maintenance of related buildings.

The establishment of Awqaf Properties Investment Fund (APIF) by The Islamic Development Bank (IsDB) in 2001 aims to finance the development of waqf real estate properties. The focus is on the properties to be invested for the utilization of their income as per the condition(s) of the endower since this form of waqf would be conducive to repaying the financing from the income of the property itself. As a fund that distributes dividends, APIF brings an element of impact investment to encourage resource mobilization for waqf.

Finally, the evolution of technology has now transformed the business environment into a more dynamic one, including Islamic finance. The Islamic finance industry is certainly no exception to the technological revolution that challenges today's Islamic financial practice norms. The integration of these technologies, when explored to the optimum, can provide the solution to the socio-economic issues underlying the problem of access to basic services. It opens the opportunity for waqf instruments to contribute. Fintech may be able to provide a significant solution. In accelerating the integration of this technology into the creation of solutions based on Islamic financial instruments, the role of scholars must be strengthened in enhancing the mastery of technology so that these pioneering solutions can achieve the desired sustainability goals. Thus, the integration of technology in the implementation of social financial instruments can not only ensure a more efficient and orderly execution but also contribute to strengthening Islamic finance in the future.

4. Exploring waqf practices in Southeast Asia

This chapter highlights waqf practices in selected Southeast Asia countries, especially collaborations related to waqf practices. An interesting fact about Southeast Asia is the strong and intact bonds and relations between the countries. Thus, the objective of this chapter is to show readers how waqf has been implemented in those selected Southeast Asia countries.

Southeast Asia has two distinctive geographic regions: First, Mainland Southeast Asia, which includes Cambodia, Laos, Myanmar (Burma), Thailand, Vietnam, and West Malaysia (Peninsular Malaysia); and second, the Indo-Malay Archipelago, which includes: Brunei, East Malaysia, all the islands of Indonesia, the Philippines, Singapore, and Timor-Leste (East Timor). It is home to multiracial groups with diverse beliefs and regions where Islam is the majority religion. According to Pew Research Centre (2009), 60 per cent of the global Muslim population is in Asia. Principally, there are 11 countries in Southeast Asia with Indonesia having the highest Muslim population, followed by Brunei, Malaysia, Singapore, Thailand, the Philippines, Myanmar, Cambodia, East Timor, Vietnam, and Laos. However, there is a bond/connection between these countries as they are neighbors.

This chapter will begin with a brief look at the selected countries, followed by the information on the Muslim population. Next, the presence of waqf development in that country will be presented. Finally, this chapter will highlight how waqf is operated in the countries of Southeast Asia and the relationships and cooperation among the neighboring Muslim countries.

INDONESIA

Indonesia is an archipelagic country located in Southeast Asia, lying between the Indian Ocean and the Pacific Ocean. Indonesia is the largest Muslim country in the world with a Muslim population of 231 million in 2021 (worldpopulationreview.com, 2021). Waqf in Indonesia is governed by an independent body: the Indonesian Waqf Board (IWB), established in 2004. Its mandate is to develop the institutions of waqf in Indonesia. It supervises, regulates, and guides the trustee administrators (*nazirs*) in managing and developing waqf assets, and it can also dismiss and replace *nazirs*. In addition, it manages and develops waqf properties at the national and international level as well as provides policy advice to the government.

Rosadi et al. (2013) highlight that the history of waqf institutions began with the advent of Islam in Indonesia, with the proof of mosques and cemeteries as the entities of waqf designation. In Indonesia, the institution and development of waqf have gone through various stages during the sultanate, colonial, independence, and reform eras. The development of waqf management in Indonesia can be categorized according to three phases. Qurrata et al. (2019) state that the first is traditional waqf; which refers to religious purposes (the existence of waqf has not provided a broader social contribution – only for community benefits). The second is the semi-professional era, where the empowerment of waqf improved. An example of the improvement of waqf activities in this era is the construction of a mosque located in a strategic location with the construction of a meeting room inside, cultivating waqf land for agriculture, and, the existence of small businesses even though the management style is still traditional. The third is the professional period that empowers the community productively. For example, in management, human resources, or cooperation (money and securities).

Starting from the first to the third phase in the development of waqf, waqf regulations went through different interpretations until the government formed waqf regulations under Act Number 41 of 2004. There are 11 chapters and 71 articles in Act Number 41 of 2004. The Act contains the necessity of waqf empowerment as a religious institution, has economic potential, promotes public welfare, and regulates waqf implementation, including the permissibility of waqf movable property, whether in the form of money, shares, securities, or others. Pertiwi et al. (2019) stated that the waqf rules are mentioned in two regulations. The first is in Law Number 41 of 2004 and the second is Government Regulation Number 42 of 2006 as an implementing regulation.

Two administrations support this Act, No 41 of 2004: (i) the Minister of Religious Affairs, to entrust waqf money and is entitled to issue a Certificate of Endowments/Waqf; and (ii) the Indonesian Waqf Board (IWB), which was established in 2004. Its mandate is to develop the institution of waqf in Indonesia. It supervises, regulates, and guides the trustee administrators (*nazirs*) in managing and developing waqf assets, and it can also dismiss and replace nazirs. In addition, it manages and develops waqf properties at the national and international level and provides policy advice to the government. Rosadi et al. (2013) add that this Act was introduced based on two considerations: (i) to promote general welfare that leads to economic benefits, and (ii) the practice of waqf that occurs in society had not been fully run orderly and efficiently. The following will explain how Act No 41 of 2004 affected the waqf practices in Indonesia.

Hasan & Ahmad (2017) mention two common or traditional practices of waqf contribution among Muslims in Indonesia. The first practice is *sadaqah*, or waqf, in the form of a small amount of charity. The second is waqf land, or a practice that combines cash waqf and waqf land. Currently, Deloitte Indonesia (2021) records that waqf in Indonesia mainly focuses on land, religious schools, and cemeteries.

However, many people still view waqf as hibah (gift) or sadaqah. According to the Indonesian Ministry of National Planning (2018), the community is aware of waqf practices but has less knowledge of the terminologies of contemporary waqf. The concept of contemporary waqf, such as cash waqf, is relatively new compared with the two traditional practices. Thus, the government takes initiatives by establishing the IWB and collaborating with Dompet Dhuafa Republika (DDR) to enhance the waqf program and change community beliefs.

One of the government approaches to diversifying the contemporary waqf practices is the Indonesia Islamic Economic Masterplan (IIEM) 2019–2024. The IIEM aims to develop the one-stop halal concept through the four strategies: (i) strengthening the halal value chain, (ii) strengthening the Islamic financial sector, (iii) strengthening micro, small–medium enterprises, and (iv) utilizing and strengthening the digital economy. The waqf practices are discovered from these strategies in the programs and activities with stakeholder participation. The main stakeholders involved in waqf practices are the Ministry of Religion, Ministry of Economic Affairs, Bank of Indonesia, Ministry of National Development Planning, and Ministry of Finance. Other agencies, such as Indonesia Ulama Council, Hajj Financial Management Body, National Defence Agency, Association Industry, and Community Organizations support as a Regulator of the IIEM. Below, we explain the waqf programs and activities in the IIEM.

The waqf programs and activities in the IIEM are discussed in its Chapter 3: Strengthening Halal Value Chain; Chapter 4: Strengthening Islamic Finance; Chapter 5: Strengthening MSME and Chapter 7: Supporting ecosystem. In Strengthening Halal Value Chain – Chapter 3 of the IIEM, focus is on six selected clusters. The clusters are:

1. Halal food and agriculture
2. Modest fashion (Muslim fashion industry)
3. Halal pharmaceutical and cosmetics
4. Halal tourism and travel and halal recreation
5. Media
6. Renewable energy

The waqf is targeted to contribute to the National Halal Media and Recreation Cluster development. In this cluster, waqf is stated in Strategy 6: easy access and financing from financial institutions or non-financial institutions and investment. The need for the waqf contribution in the halal media cluster is an investment to introduce the Islamic nuances in terms of stories inspired by Islamic values.

There are more waqf programs and activities highlighted in Chapter 4 of the IIEM. In this chapter, Strengthening Islamic Finance, four aspects are discussed: (i) Islamic banking, (ii) Islamic capital market, (iii) Social security, and (iv) Zakat and waqf. In Islamic banking, the role of waqf is as a crowdfund to support the development of the halal industry through the National Halal Fund. The fund uses a financing level subsidy by giving funds to Islamic bank customers who are developing the halal industry and fulfilling the terms of the financing provision.

In the Islamic capital market, waqf is linked to Sukuk based on the Indonesian Waqf Agency and the Ministry of Finance initiative. The Indonesian Waqf Board (IWB), as the coordinator, has the role of collecting temporary waqf funds from philanthropic institutions across Indonesia. IWB then requested the issuance of sovereign Sukuk through a special placement (private placement) to the Ministry of Finance after the funds collected reached the minimum Sukuk issuance limit. All temporary waqf funds collected at the beginning of the issuance will be returned to the wakif when the Sukuk is due.

Waqf management in Indonesia is regulated by Law No. 41 of 2004 on Waqf. According to the IIEM report, the realization of waqf funds among Muslims in Indonesia is still relatively low. However, the completion of the collection of immovable waqf objects is currently relatively high. As of 2016, waqf land in Indonesia reached 435,768 land plots with an area of 4.2 million hectares, of which around 66 per cent had waqf certificates. Thus, IIEM proposes three strategies for the waqf development plan:

a.   increasing the awareness of wakif and the society about waqf. The strategy will focus on enhancing public awareness to engage in waqf, promote waqf via various media, and conduct joint movements in cash waqf, such as the daily purchase of merchant products via e-cash or credit;

b.   strengthening the waqf ecosystem through the establishment of a technology-based waqf R&D management ecosystem, and improving the quality of Nazir as human resources by enforcing certification for waqf nazir;

c.   strengthening institutional integration of zakat institutions by establishing a standardized and integrated national waqf governance ecosystem.

Overall, the IIEM presented shows that the government of Indonesia is entirely concerned about waqf practices. In other words, IIEM shows the connection between the halal chain in every aspect of the roles of waqf and how waqf can contribute to economic growth comprehensively.

Besides the IIEM approach, Candra & Ab Rahman (2010) describe the most well-known non-Government institution – Dompet Dhuafa Republika (DDR). Dompet Dhuafa Republika is one of the nazir institutions in Indonesia, performing well in managing waqf assets, and is well-known among the Muslim community in Indonesia. According to Candra & Ab Rahman (2010), the management of endowment assets, zakat, sadaqah, and waqf (ZISWAF), is managed by both Government and non-Government institutions. Government institutions that manage these assets are usually known as the Zakat Amil Body (BAZ), while the non-Government institutions are called the Zakat Amil Board (LAZ).

There are many Zakat Amil Body and Zakat Amil Board institutions in Indonesia, and DDR is one of the non-Government institutions. DDR was recognized as a waqf foundation by the Indonesian Republic's Social Ministry on 14 September 1994. In addition, DDR is also a pioneer of waqf liquid asset management in Indonesia. DDR created a division called the Indonesian Waqf Fund (IWF) in 2005 to act as DDR's Waqf nazir, charged with developing waqf assets. Candra &Ab Rahman's (2010) study shows that the waqf assets from DDR are invested in the banking institution, Baitul Mal Wal Tamwil (BMT), and used as capital for the needy involved in SMEs based on the mudarabah and musharakah contracts. Thus, DDR is one of the important non-Government organizations contributing to waqf programs and activities. In addition, DDR has also been mentioned in IIEM as raising productive waqf funds through investments in Islamic mutual funds (Indonesian Ministry of National Planning, 2018).

In addition, Indonesia proposes IIEM to strengthen waqf roles in developing Halal industries. However, Indonesia faces challenges in managing waqf land. The issues of waqf land are reported in IIEM, which mentions that the use of waqf land is mainly for mosques (75 per cent), education (14 per cent), funerals (5 per cent), and others (6 per cent). Similarly, Deloitte Indonesia (2021) stated that waqf in Indonesia primarily focuses on lands, religious schools, and cemeteries. In addition, Hasan & Ahmad (2017) also mentioned two common or traditional practices of waqf contributions among Muslims in Indonesia. The first practice is sadaqah, or waqf, in the form of a small amount of charity. The second is waqf land, and a practice that combines cash waqf and waqf land.

Thus, establishing the Indonesian Waqf Fund (IWF) in DDR is essential to strengthening waqf management in Indonesia. Candra & Ab Rahman (2010) stated that IWF is an independent unit branch of Dompet Dhuafa Republika and acts as a statutory body foundation. The statutory body is involved in the social, education, community, and Islamic religion fields. The institution has a mission to encourage the ummah's economic development and optimize the role of waqf in the social sector and increase economic productivity.

In this aspect, waqf land is part of the waqf received by IWF to be managed. Generally, IWF's types of waqf assets are (i) non-movable waqf assets and (ii) movable waqf assets.

The example of non-movable waqf assets includes real estate or ownership of the real estate, building or part of a building, crops, ownership of accommodation according to the prevailing law, and other non-movable assets in line with Shariah and the prevailing law. An example of fixed assets is waqf assets that can benefit the community and be utilized for projects and be distributed to mawquf' alayh (waqf recipients). This is done to avoid spending on waqf assets while its benefits or returns are still unclear.

Movable waqf assets include cash, jewelry (such as gold, silver, and so on), valuable notes, vehicles, intellectual rights, rights over rents, and other movable assets following the Shariah law and the prevailing law.

IWF initiates a new approach to managing the waqf land, which in this part refers to waqf assets. Based on Candra & Ab Rahman's (2010) perspective, waqf assets are defined as changing the way we manage the assets, from consumption to production, and continuously generating returns in the future for the benefit of the waqf beneficiaries. In principle, waqf assets become the capital the moment they are bequeathed as waqf. Waqf assets remain bequeathed forever and the beneficiary can gain the benefits from waqf assets forever. From an economic perspective, Candra & Ab Rahman (2010) added that waqf assets should be invested so that the return from the investment of these assets continues to generate benefits for the beneficiaries, which can be used to provide free education and health needs, alleviation of poverty and creation of jobs.

The waqf assets managed by IWF are in cash waqf form, which can be distributed to various commercial and innovative investments. Generally, IWF invests in equity participation using mudarabah or musharakah, then IWF invests in the community's economic development.

The emergence of cash waqf globally, particularly in the Republic of Turkey, has attracted the interest and attention of the government of Indonesia. Before 2001, cash waqf was not recognized as an effective tool for waqf enhancement. However, due to the growing appetite for, and application of, cash waqf globally, the government of Indonesia realized that cash waqf is a relevant mechanism to augment and sustain waqf institutions. Upon this realization, the religious authorities issued a *fatwa* allowing the application of cash waqf.

Concerning waqf management, the law has introduced standards regarding the qualification and efficacy of waqf managers. Whether they are individuals, organizations, or corporations, they are required to demonstrate a certain level of competence and faithfulness. In terms of waqf asset securitization, the law requires that all waqf entities be certified before being able to monitor and govern the waqf assets. It also mandates the appointment of qualified legal personnel to attend to disputes that may arise involving waqf assets. Further developments took place in 2006 with the introduction of Government Regulation 42/2006, which extended the waqf asset class to include movable assets other than cash, such as capital market instruments.

Although Indonesia faces challenges with a lack of public understanding of waqf, with a high Muslim population in Indonesia, efforts to elevate the practice of waqf should be commended.

BRUNEI DARUSSALAM

Brunei is a small equatorial country on the northern coast of the island of Borneo in Southeast Asia. Islam is the official religion of Brunei Darussalam; according to a report by the Department of Economic Planning and Statistics (2021), the total population in Brunei is 429,999. There is no record of the Muslim population in the report, however, according to the Ministry of Foreign Affairs (2018), about 66 per cent of the total population is Muslim. The waqf history in Brunei has existed since the beginning of the Brunei Sultanate. Abu Bakar et al. (2020) state that waqf is performed traditionally, in which a waqif endows a property to a community leader who later acts as a nazir (trustee). The development of the waqf management in Brunei Darussalam began in 1955 with the introduction of Brunei Darussalam National Law and the 77th Judicial Circuit Courts.

In Brunei, waqf is placed under the management of the Brunei Islamic Religious Council (MUIB) that has the authority to make regulations that will be used to determine the direction of Islamic religion in Brunei Darussalam. Hasan & Ahmad (2017) state that in managing and administering the affairs of waqf property, MUIB applies the provisions of the law as enshrined in the Laws of Brunei Darussalam (Laws of Brunei), namely the Islamic Religious Council and Kadi Courts Act (Chapter 77). The Islamic Religious Council Act and Kadi Courts Act (Chapter 77) require that the Council be the sole trustee of all waqf, whether general endowment or special endowment, as in Chapter 100 of the Act.

The Act also provides that any trust, endowment or vow, affecting the terms of this Act shall be held by the Council in trust for such charitable purposes to support and expand Islam, or for the benefit of Islam in Brunei Darussalam in accordance with Islamic law as deemed fit by the Council from time to time.

Chapter 98 of the Islamic Religious Council and Kadi Courts Act (Chapter 77) states:

> The ruling provides that His Majesty the Sultan and Yang Di-Pertuan of Brunei Darussalam can give directions to the Council, not inconsistent with Islamic law or the conditions of this Act regarding the expenditure of any part of the General Endowment Fund or the income thereof, and may in the same way, cancel any of the proposed expenditures. In managing and overseeing all day-to-day management of the property donated in Brunei Darussalam, Department of Islamic Religious Council is responsible for the matter.

In addition, the Department itself has created a division called *Baitul Mal* and Endowments that oversees the affairs of waqf property and *Baitul Mal* for the Muslims in Brunei Darussalam.

In Brunei, most of the waqf contributions are in the form of properties. Generally, waqf properties in Brunei Darussalam comprise land, buildings, cash waqf for the construction of mosques, vehicles such as a hearse, religious books, holy Quran, computer equipment, air-conditioners, appliances such as mosque loudspeakers, fans, and so on (Hasan & Ahmad, 2017). Based on its position as trustee of waqf properties, the Brunei Islamic Religious Council has the power to go to any appropriate measures to manage these properties to develop and expand them to the extent permitted by Islamic law and approved by His Royal Highness the Sultan and Yang Di-Pertuan of Brunei Darussalam.

To diversify the waqf properties, Hasan & Ahmad (2017) state that the waqf properties have been developed for investment. Abu Bakar et al. (2020) examine the *Badan Tanmiah* as the investment agency body established under the Islamic Religious Council to manage the Council's property for the purpose of expanding and developing the property for the benefit of Muslims in Brunei Darussalam. The mission of *Badan Tanmiah* is to develop and enhance property through a Shariah-compliant and risk-free investment plan. Principally, there are two main functions of *Badan Tanmiah*: (i) planning and implementing the Islamic Religious Council Property Investment Plans and (ii) managing the Islamic Religious Council's real estate. As in the waqf context, *Badan Tanmiah* has managed and developed flats and houses as shops for rent. Such buildings have provided rental income to the Islamic Religious Council each month. The investment proceeds were used for the welfare of the Muslim community in Brunei Darussalam. In the meantime, Hubur (2019) also mentions that *Badan Tanmiah* develops and manages business complexes, residence buildings and gas stations. All the profits from the investments will be channeled to the poor and orphans in the form of education, health facilities and social facilities. However, the income of *Badan Tanmiah* depends on the development and investment of baitulmal lands and waqf. Low rental rates and arrears of rent that have yet to be paid by tenants have consistently caused the *Badan Tanmiah* to lack capital in planning future developments.

However, there is an effort from scholars to enhance the use of waqf land. According to Haji Puteh (2019), Brunei can benefit the use of waqf lands to enhance the country's economy, as well as relying to oil and gas revenue. Plus, waqf land is beneficial in agricultural activities to support food security and in creating job opportunities.

Thus, Abu Bakar et al. (2020) agreed that Brunei has the potential to explore and diversify the waqf activities, especially in landfill and cash waqf. Although there are lands that MUIB has successfully developed, the development is still at a minimum. There is much potential that the *Badan Tanmiah* and MUIB need to address in managing the development and investment of waqf property in Brunei.

There is no denying that Brunei presents a stronger economy and stability in society and politics. Therefore, waqf has a high potential to expand for the benefit of communities. Yaacob et al. (2020) also highlight that more research needs to be conducted to analyze the effectiveness of Islamic social finance, including waqf, in solving societal and legal challenges.

SINGAPORE

The Republic of Singapore is situated off the southern tip of the Malay Peninsula, has a diverse population of 5 million people and comprises Chinese, Malays, Indians, Caucasians and Asians of various descents. Singapore is also ranked as the fourth richest country in the world in terms of its GDP per capita. Singapore also has a large and vibrant SME community (Hasan, 2011).

The Muslim population is about 15.6 per cent of the total (Department of Statistics, Ministry of Trade and Industry, 2020). Abdul Karim (2010) explains that The Islamic Religious Council of Singapore (MUIS), under the Administration of Muslim Law Act (AMLA), governs the religious affairs of Muslims in Singapore, including the administration of waqf. AMLA also states that any person can be appointed to administer a waqf, subject to the approval of MUIS. The administration of waqf is done under the Strategy Unit of Zakat and Waqf in MUIS. All administrative and management matters concerning the selling and development of waqf assets are decided by MUIS senior management and the MUIS council.

Meanwhile, MUIS appointed two advisory panels to assist in waqf implementation. The panel comprises key players such as the Bank of Singapore, PropNex, AEP Investment, Maybank Islamic, and the National University of Singapore (Rahmad & Duriat, 2020).

Hasan (2016) states there are 101 waqf in Singapore, with 68 MUIS-managed while 33 are trustee-managed. In 2021, a total of $3.082 million was disbursed.

The largest beneficiaries were mosques, where 62 per cent was distributed to them, while madrasah disbursement was allocated 9 per cent. However, the form of the 101 waqfs is not mentioned. Nevertheless, according to Majlis Ugama Islam Singapura, MUIS (2020), waqf is managed in properties and cash. As of December 2021, waqf assets are worth more than $900 million. MUIS explains that there are two categories in waqf properties: revenue and non-revenue generating assets. Revenue-generating assets include commercial spaces and residential units.

In comparison, non-revenue generating assets consist mainly of mosques, such as Masjid Sultan and Masjid Hajjah Fatimah, and full-time madrasahs, such as Madrasah Alsagoff Al-Arabiah and Madrasah Aljunied Al-Islamiah. As for cash waqf, MUIS will invest based on shariah-compliant instruments. The net income from the investments is then channeled towards nominated beneficiaries and other shariah-compliant purposes. An example of cash waqf is Wakaf Ilmu which supports religious education.

Hasan (2016) mentions that the Strategic Zakat and Waqf Unit, the department under MUIS, oversees all waqf activities. The roles include supervising three types of waqf administrators, namely: (i) private trustees, (ii) corporate trustees, i.e., BMT, and (iii) Warees Investments Pte Ltd, i.e., MUIS waqf agents. MUIS plays the regulatory role, while the Trustees and Mutawallis play the managerial role that requires them to report and seek approval from MUIS, for example, in cases such as selling and purchasing assets.

In addition, Hasan (2016) also mentions that there are legal provisions in AMLA in sections 58 to 64 related to waqf administration. These provisions include the vesting of waqf, the registration of waqf, and the financial provision for waqf. In respect of other regulations and policies on waqf, internal procedures and workflow documents are prepared to provide general guidelines in matters relating to waqf administration. Regarding administrative excellence, MUIS has achieved ISO 9001 standard certification for its excellent management and administration of waqf. MUIS is constantly striving to enhance its management system. It has achieved the prestigious Singapore Quality Class, which marks the organization's commitment to meeting excellent standards in its processes, leadership, customer service, and result-oriented achievement.

The *zakat* and waqf strategic unit of MUIS oversees the *awqaf* administration and overall compliance with regards to the three types of waqf administrators: (i) publicly listed company – British and Malayan Trustee and BMT is a publicly listed trust company which manages some awqaf; (ii) private trustees, who manage and run awqaf set up for particular families; and (iii) a wholly-owned subsidiary of MUIS, Warees Investments Pte Ltd., which manages the rest of the awqaf. MUIS plays the regulatory role and improves the corporate governance of awqaf while the trustees and mutawallis play the managerial role and need to report and seek approval for the sale and purchase of assets. Annually, without fail, they must submit a full set of accounts to MUIS within a stipulated time following the Act. MUIS has also established a Waqf Dispute Resolution Committee. Existing *mutawallis* and trustees can choose to resolve internal disputes through mediation and, if needed, an inquiry process, without resorting to litigation. In terms of administrative striving for excellence, MUIS has achieved an ISO 9001 rating for its management and administration of awqaf.

MUIS is constantly striving to improve its excellent management systems. It has achieved certification by the Singapore Quality Institute, which marks the commitment of the organization to meeting standards of excellence in its result-oriented processes, leadership, attitude to customers, and achievements.

In Singapore, most waqf practices are in the form of waqf assets and cash waqf. However, there is a company called Finterra that manages waqf through digital technology. Below, we explain the waqf practices in Singapore.

Waqf Assets

Warees Investments Pte Ltd was established in 2002 by MUIS to manage all *awqaf* assets including tenancy matters, development, sales and purchases, and maintenance of properties. Warees receives commissions for the services it renders based on the gross income of a waqf. This incentivizes Warees to maximize returns for the *awqaf* as its income is based on the returns (Securities Commission Malaysia, 2014). Since its establishment, Warees has successfully transformed several unproductive awqaf lands into huge commercial/residential areas. Sukuk in Waqf assets include Sukuk *musharakah* for the development of an old mosque in Bencoolen Street, Singapore.

In Singapore, Sukuk *musharakah* was introduced for developing commercial buildings on waqf land. This initiative was spearheaded by Warees as a subsidiary of MUIS.

Between 2001 and 2002, Warees successfully developed two pieces of waqf land in Singapore through the issuances of Sukuk *musharakah* in which US$60 million was raised. One of these was the redevelopment of an old mosque into a multi-storey complex comprising a modern mosque, a three-storey commercial building, and a full-service 12-storey apartment block with 84 units in Bencoolen Street in 2002. The financing of the project was done through the issuance of S$35 million Sukuk *musharakah*. The *musharakah* was a joint venture among three parties, i.e. MUIS (*baitulmal*), Warees, and MUIS (Waqf). The Sukuk was fully subscribed by institutional investors. The structures of this Sukuk issuance of the redevelopment through partnership and distribution of return are described in Securities Commission Malaysia (2014).

Cash Waqf

The source of financing is mainly cash waqf contributed monthly by Muslims in Singapore. All *awqafs* are vested under MUIS. Currently, there are 140 waqf properties and 84 waqf accounts, of which 64 waqf properties and 60 waqf accounts are being managed by MUIS while another 76 waqf properties and 24 waqf accounts are managed by other mutawallis. MUIS appoints *mutawallis* to privately manage *awqaf* and approve any development or redevelopment or purchases by them. It holds the title deeds of all, including the privately managed *awqafs*. The progressive regulatory changes taken by MUIS have provided a conducive environment for financial innovation. These include allowing the leasing of waqf property for up to 99 years without transferring the ownership to the lessee and also permitting the sale of waqf properties completely and replacing them with new, higher-yielding freehold properties (*istibdal*).

Sukuk *Musharakah*

A prime example is the Sukuk *musharakah* issued by MUIS in 2002 to finance the redevelopment of an old mosque on Bencoolen Street into a multi-use complex comprising a modern mosque, a three-storey commercial building, and a fully serviced 12-storey apartment block with 84 units. Sukuk *musharakah* has allowed investors in Singapore and abroad to participate directly in developing various waqf assets. Between 2001 and 2002, Warees raised $SGD60 million through the issuances of Sukuk *musharakah* to develop two Waqf lands in Singapore (Al-Haddad & Suleman, 2021). Additionally, the amendment of AMLA to establish a sinking fund for waqf will allow better budgetary planning for the upkeep and development of waqf properties.

Fintech

One of the leading technology-based companies providing blockchain-based Islamic applications that address global issues, Finterra, was established in 2017 and currently has a presence in Malaysia, Singapore, Hong Kong, UAE, and India, with plans to further expand into Africa and the rest of the Middle East. Globally, Finterra promotes community growth and advocates for the mass adoption of groundbreaking blockchain technology, serving as a "Social Solution for Blockchain". Its ecosystem comprises core banking, digital banking, and blockchain solutions that have been developed to bridge the gap between users, merchants, and financial institutions.

The Finterra ecosystem offers a truly inclusive platform to consumers through various verticals, including an Open Source Development platform, e-Commerce platform, and an environment that supports the development of Islamic Social Finance. Finterra's flagship product, the WAQFChain has been developed to revitalize the Islamic Social Economic system for the digital age using blockchain technology. With relevant regulatory compliance built into the product, the WAQFChain solves core challenges in unlocking and integrating options for capital raising, waqf management, and asset management. According to Mohd Zain et al. (2019), good practice can be learned from a waqf crowdfunding company like Finterra where they have their Shariah experts that work as their Shariah advisors in providing advice and ensuring that their crowdfunding is consistent with the principles of Shariah. Rahmad & Duriat (2020) add that Finterra also has signed an MoU with the IsDB's arm to leverage each other's strengths to achieve sustainable business growth. The details of how Finterra works is explained in Chapter 6.

Rahmad & Duriat (2020) reported that the challenges in the Singapore scenario are because of the market size limitation even though Singapore has succeeded as an international fintech hub. In addition, acceptance of Islamic financial instruments in Singapore is low, and its regulators do not intend to promote Islamic finance as mainstream.

THAILAND

According to Mohd Zain et al. (2019), Muslims in Thailand are the second largest minority, with a majority of them located in four southern provinces: Patani, Narathiwat, Yala, and Satul. They are living in the area near the Northern part of the Malay Peninsula. Moreover, the Muslims in those four provinces in the South are not an immigrant community, but indigenous to the area. They are categorized as Malay-Muslim communities. Being a non-Muslim country, Thailand does not have any law specifically governing the needs of waqf and *zakat* institutions. Mustafa et al. (2021) state that Thailand has about 64 million people. Of the total, about 7.5 million are Muslims, about 12 per cent of the total Thai population.

Currently, waqf in those four provinces is run under the supervision of the Provincial Islamic Committee and mosque committees. Thai laws concerning waqf properties and the practices of waqf committees in the Malay-Muslim majority areas focus on the practices of Al-Muhammadi Mosque Waqf Committee (AMWC). Therefore, the following section, based on Dorloh's (2015) review of waqf institutions in Thailand, will discuss the following: (i) the method of collecting waqf property, (ii) Thai law related to the affairs of Muslims in Thailand, and (iii) the Royal Act on people Islam Mosque 1947.

Method of Collecting Waqf Properties

The common practice in collecting waqf property in these areas is that the contributor will donate or dispose of his land to the mosque. The recipient will be
the *imam*. In most cases, the trustee for waqf property is the mosque committee
itself. The waqf properties in the Malay-Muslim areas comprise open land,
apartments and rubber or coconut plantations. All these properties are donated
to mosques. Incomes from these properties would go to the maintenance of
mosques and religious schools. The balance would be deposited in waqf committee's account. The objective of collecting waqf property is to bring waqf
properties towards sustainable development and poverty alleviation.

Laws Concerning Muslim Affairs in Thailand

In Thailand, all religious matters including waqf, collecting *zakat*, and *fitrah*
are administered jointly by Chularajmontri (*Shaykh al-Islam*), Provincial
Committee for Islamic Affairs (PCIA), and Mosque Committee Member
(MCM). The position of waqf land in Thailand is out of the ambit of Thai civil
law. Fortunately, there has been a decided case by the Narathiwat Provincial
Court (NPC) as to the recognition of waqf property under Islamic law. Those
laws are as follows.

The Royal Act concerning Muslim Mosque, 1947
As stated in the Muslim Mosque Act 1947, the MCM has been given the
duty and power to manage and administer the affairs of the mosque and its
property according to Islamic law and the law of the country. In addition,
their responsibility is to ensure the proper observance of Islam according to
the Malay culture. By this Act, the MCM is formed. Before the committees
are appointed, the mosque must be first registered at the Muslim Religious
Committee Council (MRCC) in the respective province.

   Indeed, many mosques in Thailand are unregistered and are not eligible for
the government's subsidiary and legal recognition. The details of the mosque
as to its location, MCM, the letter of the appointment of *imam, khatib*, and *bilal*
must be verified by MRCC. The verified document will be submitted to the
provincial governor. The appointment and dismissal of the *imam, khatib*, and
bilal are usually made by the MRCC, subject to the consent of the community
in that area. However, the Internal Affairs Ministry is entrusted to monitor the
appointment of the Mosque Committee Members who are obedient to the state
(Dorloh, 2015).

   The job scope of the MCM is stated clearly in the Royal Act concerning
Muslim Mosque, 1947. Dorloh (2015) lists the numbers of registered mosques
as follows: Patani with 544 mosques; Narathiwat (477 mosques); Yala (308

mosques); and Satul (147 mosques). Hence, Dorloh (2015) suggests that waqf implementation in Thailand should consider the following.

- Accepting Shariah as part of Thai laws. The possibility of making Shariah a source of Thai law is based on the decisions of the Thai judges in the case of Al-Muhammadi waqf property.
- As none of the Thai National Land Code (TNLC) provisions and other laws is devoted to Waqf land, the only way lands can be dedicated for waqf by Muslims is through the mechanisms of Islamic law of waqf, mechanisms that are being implemented by the Islamic Religious Councils in these four areas.
- Since there is no waqf legislation in Thailand, this will be problematic. Thus, there is a dire need for a new and complete law for waqf. If the law could not be passed by the parliament, the call for the establishment of an independent body or board which is responsible to regulate waqf institutions should be considered by the Thai government.

Even though Thailand has a significant gap in practicing Islamic social finance compared with neighboring countries, the existing practices of waqf have attracted non-Muslims to understand the benefits of philanthropies.

THE PHILIPPINES

The Philippines is also located in Southeast Asia. The US Department of State (2021) reported that approximately 6 per cent of the population is Muslim, according to the Philippine Statistics Authority (PSA), while the National Commission on Muslim Filipinos (NCMF) estimates a figure of 10 to 11 per cent. The NCMF attributes its higher estimate to several factors, including the reluctance of Muslims to officially register with the civil registrar office or to participate in the formal survey, the community's transience due to internal movement for work, and the government's failure to survey Muslim areas and communities thoroughly.

According to the PSA, approximately 4 per cent of those surveyed in the 2015 census did not report a religious affiliation or belonged to other faiths, such as animism or indigenous syncretic faiths. A majority of Muslims are members of various ethnic minority groups and reside in Mindanao and nearby islands in the south. Muslims constitute a majority in the Bangsamoro Autonomous Region in Muslim Mindanao (BARMM). An increasing number of Muslims are migrating to the urban centers of Manila, Baguio, Dumaguete, Cagayan de Oro, Iligan, Cotabato, and Davao, a trend that accelerated after the May–October 2017 siege of Marawi, during which residents fled to other provinces for their security. According to Mohd Shukri et al. (2019), Marawi

City, situated in the southern island of Mindanao in the Philippines has been known as a spiritual and cultural center of the Muslims in that state. Marawi City has been known as the only "Islamic city" of the Philippines, for having many beautiful mosques and schools in every district of the city.

Most of the mosques and schools were built on waqf lands and financed by cash waqf contributed by individuals and religious private organizations. There are also waqf properties dedicated to community services such as health services, water systems, shelter, and others.

From the Murat Cizakca writing, the Muslims of the Philippines were left free to establish their waqf according to their customs and beliefs. The waqf establishment is subject to the Philippine Corporation Law, a secular body of law adopted during the American occupation. Property rights, on the other hand, are governed by the Philippine Civil Code, a reproduction of the Spanish Code. There are also a few pertinent Articles in the Code of Muslim Personal Law (Cizakca, 2021). The growth of waqf activities in the Philippines can be seen through establishment of the Islamic Trust and Development Foundation. It helps mobilize waqf activities in the surrounding area. A voluntary organization named *Markazos Shabab Al-Muslim fil-Filibin*, located in the province of Lanao, acts as the sole administrator of waqf property. According to Cizakca (2021), Muslims are encouraged to donate to the *Markazos* that use these funds to construct and maintain mosques, schools, and other charitable institutions.

Cizakca (2021) adds some families endow (waqf) their assets. The most famous family endowment example is *Jami'atul Philippine al-Islamiyah*, a prominent family established in Marawi City, Philippines. It has established the only Islamic university in the country populated exclusively by Muslim students. It has established the only Islamic university in the country that is populated exclusively by Muslim students. Since part of the net income accrues to the founder's family, the waqf does not enjoy tax exemption. The waqf has a juridical personality and is managed by a board that is chaired by the eldest son of the founder.

However, Mohd Shukri et al. (2019) claimed there had been changes in the waqf development in Marawi City after 2017. The waqf lands used for the masjid (mosque), madrasah (school), water system, dormitories, and other charitable properties were mostly part of ancestral lands converted to waqf properties as agreed upon or with the consent of the members of the respective family. These waqf properties gave something that the government of the Philippines failed to provide to the Muslim minority. Waqf has become the only financial source for Muslim scholars to produce research output that contributes to the development of the Muslim culture and activities in the Philippines.

At the same time, Mohd Shukri et al. (2019) mentioned that the Islamic bond (Sukuk) has been considered as part of Philippine President Rodrigo

Duterte's "Build, Build, Build" program to fund infrastructure projects. According to Romeo Montenegro, the director of Mindanao Development Authority (MinDA), the Islamic finance recovery scheme for Marawi is viable if a general framework for the Islamic finance ecosystem is in place. The development of the Islamic finance industry in the Philippines is still at its early stages as there is only one Islamic bank in the country – Al Amanah Islamic Investment Bank of the Philippines, which does not operate as a fully-fledged Islamic bank.

COLLABORATION OF WAQF AMONG SOUTHEAST ASIA COUNTRIES

Myanmar, Cambodia, East Timor, Vietnam, and Laos have the least Muslim populations recorded in 2021.

In Myanmar, a report from The World Population Review estimates that the Muslim population is about 4.3 per cent of the total 54 million population (World population review, 2021). Nu Htay et al. (2013) mention that waqf (as one of the Islamic social finances), can be of benefit to non-Muslims even though Muslims are a minority in Myanmar.

Cambodia is surrounded by three other Southeast Asian countries as well as a main body of water. Thailand lies to the upper northwest of Thailand, while Laos is to the northeast. Cambodia shares both its eastern and southern borders with Laos. The Gulf of Thailand can be found along the western coastline of Cambodia. Over 95 per cent of the population practices Theravada Buddhism, the official religion, with an estimated 4,400 monastery temples in the country. Islam is the main religion of the majority of Malay and Chams minorities in the country, while most Muslims are Sunnis. There are approximately 300,000 Muslims in Cambodia, with about 1 per cent identified as Christian (World population review, 2021).

In East-Timor or Timor-Leste, the US government estimated the total population was at 1.3 million (July 2018 estimate). According to the 2015 census, 97.6 per cent of the population were Catholic, 1.96 per cent were Protestant, and less than 1 per cent were Muslim. Protestant denominations include the Assemblies of God, Baptists, Presbyterians, Methodists, Seventh-day Adventists, Pentecostals, Jehovah's Witnesses, and the Christian Vision Church. There are also several small nondenominational Protestant congregations. Many citizens also retain animistic beliefs and practices along with their monotheistic religious affiliation (US Department of State, 2018).

In Vietnam, the US Department of State (2020b) stated that approximately 80,000 Muslims are scattered throughout the country. Authorities permitted Catholic, Protestant, Muslim, Baha'i, and Buddhist groups to provide religious education to adherents in their facilities, and religious leaders have noted increased enrollment in these education programs in recent years.

For Laos, the US Department of State (2020a) reported a small number of Muslims: approximately 1,000 people.

WAQF DEVELOPMENT AT PRESENT

There are limited sources of how waqf is developing in Laos, Myanmar, Vietnam, East Timor or Timor-Leste, and Cambodia. Most of the Southeast Asia countries that have large Muslim populations actively participate via NGOs to contribute to countries with smaller Muslim populations. It is recorded that most of the waqf is through waqf crowdfunding. For example, in Malaysia, waqaftelaga.com contributes to eight countries including Myanmar, Vietnam, and Cambodia. In the Philippines, kitafund.com provides medical and humanitarian needs and emergency aid by collecting through crowd-funding. In Indonesia, kitabisa.com operates similarly through crowdfunding. Generally, besides providing a well and water pump for a small Muslim village in the country, the NGO also provides a proper waqf toilet, waqf motorcycle for Ustaz to teach Islam in the community, support education fees for the needy, etc.

For Myanmar, there is one study by Nu Htay et al. (2013) that mentions the waqf clinic named Myint Myat Phu Zin, which is located in the middle of Mandalay, Myanmar. This is the first clinic operating based on the integration of the waqf, *zakat*, and *sadaqah*. This clinic is for the benefit of both Muslims and non-Muslims as it is operated through the collection from Muslims (*zakat*, *sadaqah* and waqf) and non-Muslims (charity).

Waqf contributions, as an Islamic social financial tool, play an important role in Southeast Asia's Muslim community. Most of the waqf practices in Southeast Asia countries are waqf assets and cash waqf, especially in Indonesia, Brunei, Singapore, and Malaysia.

Waqf in Indonesia is governed by an independent body, the Indonesian Waqf Board and Dompet Dhuafa Republika. In Brunei, the management of waqf is by the Brunei Islamic Religious Council (MUIB), while in Singapore, The Islamic Religious Council of Singapore (MUIS), under the Administration of Muslim Law Act (AMLA), governs the religious affairs of Muslims, including the administration of waqf. In Thailand, the minority Muslims are organized by the waqf committee through the practices of the Al-Muhammadi Mosque Waqf Committee (AMWC). In the Philippines, The Islamic Trust and Development Foundation aims to promote waqf establishment among the Muslims through the voluntary organization Markazos Shabab Al-Muslim fil-Filibin. In other Southeast Asia countries, there is no Muslim Act recorded or any organization to manage waqf. However, the bonds and relationships among these Southeast Asia countries are connected through the participation of NGOs from neighboring countries.

Thus, it is understood that the role of waqf is to help the greater Muslim community participate in financial and commercial matters by putting their wealth into circulation. It does not only enable Muslims to participate in the sophisticated Islamic financial system, but also encourages all levels of society to participate in financial matters through financial inclusion such as Islamic microfinance, waqf, etc. The Islamic financial systems help to foster a safety net for society through wealth distribution and redistribution tools such as *zakat*, *ṣadaqah*, and other forms of religious contributions. Schools, hospitals, and other institutions can be built through such funds and can even fund needy students. The next chapter will explore the waqf practices in Malaysia.

5. Waqf development in Malaysia

This chapter focuses on waqf development in Malaysia. The purpose of this chapter is to present how the government of Malaysia plays its roles in achieving the objectives in waqf development. First, this chapter introduces the glimpse of waqf history in Malaysia and the establishment of the Malaysia Waqf Foundation (MWF). Then, this chapter lists contemporary waqf practiced in Malaysia including cash waqf, waqf assets, waqf investment and corporate waqf shares. Generally, the waqf development in Malaysia is divided into two: waqf governance and contemporary waqf. Currently, the contemporary waqf in Malaysia includes cash waqf, waqf assets, waqf investment, and corporate waqf. This chapter aims to present to the reader how the government of Malaysia plays a significant role in achieving the objective of waqf development. Thus, this chapter lists the objectives of waqf development in Malaysia (through SDGs) and Malaysia's initiatives in developing waqf practices to achieve the waqf objectives. Malaysia is taking the initiatives in developing waqf practices that were highlighted in the 11th Malaysia Plan (2016–2020), followed by the 12th Malaysia Plan (2021–2025) as a step to empower micro, small and medium enterprises' roles.

THE HISTORY OF WAQF DEVELOPMENT IN MALAYSIA

Mohamad Al-Bakri (2020) mentioned that the practice of waqf in Malaysia can be traced back to the Malacca Sultanate in the fifteenth century. The development of waqf properties went through remarkable changes during the colonization period by the Portuguese (1511–1641), Dutch (1641–1824), and British (1826–1946). During British rule, a series of laws were enacted in the 1950s (Perak in 1951 and 1965; Selangor in 1952; Terengganu in 1955; Malacca in 1959; and Johor in 1978) which drastically centralized the Malaysian waqf system.

Since then, Ibrahim and Ibrahim (2013) elaborate that all the 14 states in Malaysia have been placed under the power of the Sultan who is given full authority by the Federal Government to manage all religious matters, which include *zakat*, *baitulmal*, waqf, and others. The Sultan, then, passed on the power to the State Islamic Religious Council (SIRC) of each state in Malaysia to oversee all religious matters.

THE ESTABLISHMENT OF MALAYSIA WAQF FOUNDATION

Md Saad et al. (2017) state that in the Federal constitution, the responsibility of waqf management is placed under the respective SIRC. On March 27, 2004, the government of Malaysia established the Department of *Wakaf, Zakat*, and *Hajj* (JAWHAR) to monitor the effectiveness and efficiency of waqf, *zakat*, and *hajj* administration in every state in Malaysia. JAWHAR's role is to create a standard system in the financial management of the SIRCs, to establish and coordinate a standard ICT application at SIRCs, to monitor the management and development of waqf properties, to give advice and facilitate organizational development and matters relating to waqf, to conduct research, prepare reports and present statements on waqf issues, to organize coordinating meetings and conferences about waqf and to represent the country in consultation and official forums related to waqf.

In realizing these functions, multiple initiatives have been taken, such as the formation of the JAWHAR Code of Ethics in 2007, the publication of the Waqf Land Management Manual in 2006, the development of the e-waqf system in 2007, and the formation of Malaysia Waqf Foundation (MWF) in 2008, which aim to enhance and improve the efficiency of waqf management.

Malaysia Waqf Foundation (MWF) is a national endowment entity under JAWHAR and was established on July 23, 2008 through the Trustee (Incorporation) Act 1952 (Act 258).

MWF's role is to mobilize waqf resources and complement SIRC's efforts in developing waqf properties in Malaysia. The main functions of the MWF are to collect and generate funds to develop waqf properties and collaborate with the SIRCs.

The SIRCs are sole trustees for all waqf properties as specified in the Islamic legal acts/enactments in the states. As the sole trustee, the SIRCs have the authority to:

a. Appoint or give written permission to any party to manage and administer any *mawquf* on his behalf.
b. Recognize the appointment of any manager or administration in a situation where the *waqif* has already appointed himself other than SIRC.
c. Terminate the appointment according to the statements (a) and (b) above.

Table 5.1 presents the list of State Enactments relating to the administration and management of waqf in Malaysia.

There are two main types of waqf products offered by MWF: the cash waqf scheme and the building waqf certificate.

*Table 5.1   State enactments relating to the administration and
                management of waqf in Malaysia*

No	State	Enactment
1	Johor	• Enactment No.16 of 2003
		Administration of the Religion of Islam (State of Johor) Enactment 2003
2	Kedah	• Enactment 9
		Administration of Islamic Law (Kedah Darul Aman) Enactment 2008
		Incorporating Latest Amendment - KPU 29/2008
3	Kelantan	• Enactment No. 4 of 1994
		Council of the Religion of Islam and Malay Custom, Kelantan Enactment 1994
4	Melaka	• Enactment No. 7 of 2002
		Administration of The Religion of Islam (State of Malacca) Enactment 2002
		• Enactment 5
		Wakaf (State of Malacca) Enactment 2005
5	Negeri Sembilan	• Enactment No.10 of 2003
		Administration of the Religion of Islam (Negeri Sembilan) Enactment 2003
		Incorporating latest amendment – En. A12/2012
		Enactment not yet in force:
		• Enactment 2
		Wakaf (Negeri Sembilan) Enactment 2005
		Incorporating latest amendment – NSPU27/2008
6	Pahang	• Enactment No.3 of 1991
		Administration of Islamic Law Enactment 1991
		Incorporating latest amendment – En. 5/2001
7	Perak	• Enactment No.4 of 2004
		Administration of the Religion of Islam (Perak) Enactment 2004
		Incorporating latest amendment – En. A30
		Enactment not yet in force:
		• Enactment 9 of 2015
		Wakaf Enactment (Perak) 2015
8	Perlis	• Enactment No.4 of 2006
		Administration of the Religion of Islam Enactment 2006
		Incorporating latest amendment – En. A20
9	Pulau Pinang	• Enactment 2
		Administration of the Religion of Islam (State of Penang) Enactment 2004
		Incorporating latest Amendment – Pg. PU 11/2008

No	State	Enactment
10	Sabah	• Enactment No. 11 of 1998
		Baitulmal Corporation Enactment 1998
		• Enactment No.5 of 2004
		Majlis Ugama Islam Negeri Sabah Enactment 2004
11	Sarawak	• Chapter 41
		Majlis Islam Sarawak Ordinance 2001
12	Selangor	• Enactment No.1 of 2003
		Administration of the Religion of Islam (State of Selangor) Enactment 2003 *Incorporating latest amendment – En. A 25*
		• Enactment No.15 of 2015
		Wakaf (State of Selangor Waqf) Enactment 2015
13	Wilayah persekutuan	• Act 505
		Administration of Islamic Law (Federal Territories) Act 1993 *Incorporating latest amendment – PU (A) 250/2002*
14	Terengganu	• Enactment No. 2 of 2001
		Administration of Islamic Religious Affairs (Terengganu) Enactment 1422H/2001M *Incorporating latest amendment – En. A28/2012*
		• Enactment 1/2016
		Wakaf (Terengganu) Enactment 2016

Source: E-Syariah Official Portal, http://www.esyariah.gov.my

The cash waqf scheme offers five schemes: general cash waqf, waqf khas, cash waqf certificate, health cash waqf certificate, and economic development cash waqf certificate. Under these schemes, cash waqf is collected normally by MWF according to current needs, including distributing the funds to SIRC. Cash waqf can choose between these three categories which are education, health, and economic development where the proceeds of this contribution will be used for waqf development under the segment.

For the building waqf certificate, MWF will advance MWF funds (not waqf or endowment funds) to purchase buildings in strategic locations. MWF will then create units for the building to open opportunities for the public to purchase and then endow the units. Once the entire building unit is endowed, the building will be registered as a waqf asset of the SIRCs.

The waqf practices in Malaysia generally comprise three major categories: waqf am, waqf Khas, and waqf *al-mushtarak* (or *al-musytarak*). Waqf am refers to any form of waqf dedication aimed at general welfare without specifying any particular beneficiaries (individuals or organizations/institutions) or specific purposes. This category of waqf applies to things or objectives directed towards general social welfare and charitable purposes. In contrast, waqf khas is a type of waqf with specified beneficiaries or purposes. Under this form of waqf, the *waqif* will identify the persons who are to benefit from the *awqaf* or the purpose for which the waqf must be applied. The combination of waqf am and waqf khas forms the hybrid category, waqf *al-mushtarak*. An example of waqf *al-mushtarak* in Malaysia is the Setee Aishah waqf in Pulau Pinang, Malaysia (Abdul Razak, 2020).

Waqf Governance Structure in Malaysia

Historically, M. Nasir and Patria (2021) describe waqf governance based on these three types: decentralized, semi-centralized, and centralized. Decentralized waqf governance occurred during the time of the Prophet Muhammad (pbuh). The administration of waqf was decentralized, and the founder of the waqf could either administer the waqf himself or appoint a trustee to administer the waqf on his behalf. Semi-centralized waqf governance refers to the state managing and supervising waqf assets due to an increase in waqf properties.

During the times of Hisham bin Abdel Malik (684–705 AD), the Diwan Ahbas (Ministry of *Awqaf*) was created to protect waqf property from abuse. The management of public waqf was placed under the jurisdiction of the Diwan Ahbas, while the management of family waqf was left to their founders and trustees. The third type is centralized waqf governance, in which the Ministry of *Awqaf* has the authority to manage and administer all waqf property. However, the core issue of waqf governance is not the type of administration per se. Rather, it is accountability and transparency. Hence, accountability and transparency in the governance of waqf assets matters, whether the government manages cash waqf and other waqf assets directly or indirectly.

In Malaysia, waqf governance is formed based on the participation from the government (establishment of MWF in JAWHAR) and Association of Islamic Banking and Financial Institutions Malaysia (AIBIM). According to Kamaruddin and Mohd Hanefah (2021), there is no general standard on waqf governance practices in Malaysia at present. However, the AIBIM had issued a related waqf governance guidance which is the Code of Governance and Transparency for the waqf fund in 2017. In this case, although the code is specifying for Islamic banks' practices, it still can be used as guidance for other organizations involved with waqf funds, such as waqf institutions and Islamic non-profit organizations on waqf governance practices in Malaysia.

CONTEMPORARY WAQF PRACTICES IN MALAYSIA

According to Mohamad Al-Bakri (2020), contemporary waqf can be applied in the form of either dedicating real estate, furniture, fixtures, and equipment (FFE) other movable assets, or liquid forms of money and wealth such as cash and shares. Currently, in Malaysia, the contemporary waqf include cash waqf, waqf asset, Sukuk, and corporate waqf. The 2021 Budget is proof that the government of Malaysia is determined to empower the management of waqf through collaborations between MWF with Federal government agencies, GLCs, and GLICs (Mohamad Al-Bakri, 2020). The following section explains the details.

Cash Waqf

History in Malaysia shows that cash waqf was first introduced by Perak Islamic State Religious Council in 1957, followed by other SIRCs. According to Mohamed Nor and Yaakub (2015) and Mohd Thas Thaker et al. (2021), all the matters of cash waqf including waqf are governed and enacted by the SIRC of each state. Each SIRC issues its respective *fatwa* (legal opinion) regarding the permissible areas in which funds received through cash waqf can be spent or invested. The Malaysian waqf authorities have approved a cash waqf provided that it is converted into or used towards creating permanent benefits (Global Islamic Finance Report, 2015). Normally, the funds collected will be used to purchase immovable assets or be added to existing waqf development projects.

Cash waqf in Malaysia gained popularity when JAWHAR, MWF as well as Waqaf An-Nur Corporation Berhad initiated various waqf projects through the cash waqf scheme (Bakar, 2018). Waqaf An-Nur Corporation Berhad is a limited company with no share guarantee initiated by the establishment of Johor Corporation (JCorp), Malaysia (waqafannur.com.my).

Another example is a collaboration between Islamic commercial bank, Bank Muamalat Malaysia Berhad (BMMB) with four SIRCs – Selangor, Negeri Sembilan, Kedah, and Kelantan under the name of Wakaf Muamalat. The program collects cash waqf funds from the public and corporations which are used for health and education purposes including the development of infrastructure, financing health equipment, healthcare costs and fees, and education scholarships. To ensure transparency in the management of waqf funds, Wakaf Muamalat service is monitored by two auditing bodies – the internal audit position of Selangor's SIRC and the internal audit from BMMB. Management activities are audited frequently, and audit reports will be submitted to the Joint Management Authority.

Waqf Assets

Generally, a waqf asset refers to something that fulfills the syara' and the asset is required to have value (*mutaqawwīm*) whether it is an immovable asset, sam (*'aqār*), movable asset (*manqūl*), usufruct or rights of ownership (Omar et al., 2013). As mentioned in Chapter 1, the immovable property consists of land and buildings, whilst movable property refers to books, prayer mats, and even cash. In the current context, waqf from movables practicing in Malaysia includes cash waqf, waqf shares, and waqf of gold. The latter is a new kind of mawquf accepted by the Malaysia Waqf Foundation (Global Islamic Finance Report, 2015).

According to Omar et al. (2013), the development of land into commercial buildings such as supermarkets, accommodation (hotels), and residential estates are examples of new productive waqf assets. Previously, Malaysians preferred their waqf to be established from immovables, consisting of landed properties, especially for the erection of mosques, graveyards, and Islamic religious schools, including the *pondok* schools. Ibrahim and Ibrahim (2013) highlight that the management of waqf properties in Malaysia has improved tremendously. This is largely due to the clauses included in the regulation pertinent to the waqf properties:

a.   The Council of Islamic Religion or the Majlis Ugama Islam dan 'Adat Melayu is the sole trustee of all waqf properties.
b.   All documents pertaining to waqf properties must be kept by the Council.
c.   The Council must take the necessary steps to transfer the ownership of all waqf properties to itself.
d.   All moneys received from specific waqf properties must be used according to the purpose for which such properties were intended.
e.   All moneys received from general waqf properties must be kept in the general fund of the Majlis or *Bait al-mal*.

Thus, in waqf assets, the examples of waqf land management and movable waqf (waqf sukuk) are discussed.

Waqf land management
Principally, waqf land is the highest issue to be conducted. For waqf land, JAWHAR aims to develop waqf lands around Malaysia with the collaboration of the SIRCs and to establish an efficient, standard, and Shariah-compliant management for waqf institutions. An example of waqf land management in Malaysia is the commercial development of waqf assets practiced by the state Islamic religion of Pulau Pinang. According to Omar et al. (2013), the SIRC

of Pulau Pinang (IRCPP) is one of the most advanced and progressive SIRCs in Malaysia in the effort to commercially develop the waqf assets under its custody. All the terrace house lots on the Seetee Aishah waqf land have been fully booked by potential buyers. IRCPP's success is primarily due to the strategic location of the waqf land and its existing high market value. With IRCPP's expertise and also the support and cooperation by the developer, IRCPP can develop the waqf land on a large scale. The method of financing can be adapted by other trustees, as long as they get similar cooperation from financiers or investors. Given the exciting and promising real estate economic development currently, it is high time for the unproductive waqf lands to be developed, regardless of whether the waqf lands have specific or general characteristics. Development must be carried out to fulfill waqf owner's wish and at the same time takes into consideration economic return that can be beneficial to *mawqūf 'alayh.*

Waqf assets in sukuk
Technically, sukuk refers to Islamic bonds or literal certificates. This certificate is an investment in assets that use Shariah principles and concepts. Securities Commission Malaysia (2014) interprets that the investors may receive profit or income from the cash flow generated from the assets or investment in the asset in the form of periodic distributions. The returns may be fixed or variable depending on the mechanisms applied. Basically, in the Islamic capital market, sukuk plays the role of financing certain economic activities according to Shariah principles. Sukuk can be structured to meet medium to long-term financing. Securities Commission Malaysia (2014) explains that the sukuk issuance is to be used as capital raising for the development of waqf assets. Under Shariah contracts, there are four structuring sukuk: lease-based, agency-based, sale-based, and partnership-based.

Securities Commission Malaysia (2014) shares that the world's first ringgit Malaysia corporate sukuk was issued in 1990 by a Malaysian subsidiary of the Shell Group. According to Zain and Muhamad (2020), there is a potential for a Musharakah-based sukuk model to be developed and implemented in Malaysia as waqf properties or waqf assets. Musharakah-based sukuk is under a partnership-based contract structure.

Towards improving waqf services, Malaysia has introduced the Skim Saham Wakaf to be implemented by several SIRCs; for instance, Selangor's SIRC (Mohamed Nor & Yaakub, 2015). Through this concept, the SIRCs will act as a trustee and participants must buy the shares of waqf earlier, and then they endow it. The money from the shares will be collected under a special fund and will be channeled to economic, educational, and social programs dependent on the choices made by the participants.

Waqf investment

In 2020, the Securities Commission introduced the Islamic Capital Market (ICM) as a new waqf assets approach. Security Commission Malaysia (2020) had launched Waqf-Featured Unit Trust Funds to facilitate the offering of unit trust funds and wholesale funds with waqf features that integrate commercial and social objectives. Only an Islamic unit trust fund and Islamic wholesale fund that comply with the requirements are eligible to be offered in Waqf-Featured Unit Trust Funds.

One of the examples of Waqf-Featured Unit Trust Funds is Makmur myWakaf Fund. This fund is BIMB Investment Management Berhad (BIMB Investment), a wholly-owned subsidiary of Bank Islam Malaysia Berhad (BIMB). The MWF is the first waqf Featured Unit Trust Fund under the Securities Commission (SC) Malaysia. BIMB Investment is the first fund management company to structure and design a waqf unit trust fund, hence, introducing a new investment dimension into the fund management industry in Malaysia. This product combines Shariah-based principles in mobilizing funds for the betterment of society. Apart from social finance, the focus on healthcare, education, and community empowerment whilst providing investment returns for investors makes this fund truly innovative.

The MWF aims at investors who wish to channel a part of their investment returns for waqf purposes to underprivileged communities in the mentioned focused sectors in Malaysia. The MWF aims to distribute monthly income distribution, subject to availability of income, and channel 50 per cent of the income distribution for waqf purposes through AIBIM's myWakaf initiative. A Half-Yearly Waqf Asset Report will be featured in the Fund's interim and annual reports, from which, unit holders will be informed on the distribution of the waqf asset.

WAQF SHARES

Waqf shares are different from waqf of shares. In this context, waqf shares are invested shares producing profit, and the profit is used to finance waqf activities instead of giving it as dividends to investors (Ambrose et al., 2015).

Abdel Mohsin (2012) adds the concept of waqf shares as fundraising to improve and to upgrade the current situation of these properties so that they can deliver the suspected services needed in the different societies. One of the examples introduced in Pahang, Malaysia is the Pahang Waqf Shares Scheme. This scheme is open to the public according to the sale method of waqf share units with a value of RM10 per unit. Through the sale of these shares, a waqf fund is created and the waqf funds accumulated in the Pahang Saham Trust Fund Waqf Account will finance further projects or those planned by the management. One form of activity financed from this account is for Islamic education, such as Maahad Tahfiz school in Pahang and Fardhu Ain study classes. Abdel Mohsin (2012) asserts that the main objectives in supporting such a scheme are to inculcate the culture of creating waqf, to provide an alternative and platform for Muslims to be involved in waqf, to encourage the Muslim society to recognize waqf as a viable tool to enhance the economic position of the ummah, and to encourage Muslims to cooperate under the concept of cooperation.

Corporate Waqf Shares

There are various views explaining how corporate waqf arrangement is carried out. Saad (2019) states that the involvement of corporate waqf can be through (i) a majority owner of a company that exercises managerial control, or (ii) a minority shareholder that exercises minority voting rights.

Many agree that Johor Corporation's (JCorp) is the first Malaysian corporate company to emerge as the corporate waqf management (Omar et al., 2018) in 2006. The Malaysian government has stepped forward to develop more waqf institutions by proposing a Corporate Waqf Master Plan, as announced in the 2013 Budget. The plan could help unleash the potential for waqf, corporate waqf, in particular, to be another growth driver for the Islamic financial industry. A corporate waqf platform that is professionally managed has the ability to attract broader participation from the waqif, or donors, given its legal and governance structure that would provide a higher degree of confidence to the market (Mar Iman & Haji Mohammad, 2017). Aligned with the establishment of the Corporate Waqf Master Plan, the Malaysian Accounting Standard Board (MASB) participates in checking the accounting process in waqf management (Malaysian Accounting Standards Board, 2014).

Looking at the roles of a corporate company, waqf activities are not about financial support only but are also designed to facilitate solving environmental problems by each community in order to achieve societal development. There are many ways and forms that can be presented as waqf. It can be in the form of rental of waqf properties and cultivation of waqf lands and being permitted to make profits for waqf for the purpose of creating wealth useful for the poor or needy (Mar Iman & Haji Mohammad, 2017). Waqf can provide non-financial support for the smaller enterprise and the most common contribution is in the land. For example, UDA Holdings and the waqf lands in Indonesia are also being utilized for other benefits such as farming activities, shop lots, and rice factories.

The second example is adopting waqf institutions by entering into partnership contracts with entrepreneurs. According to Osman et al. (2015), Majlis Agama Islam Kedah (MAIK) was used as a method to upgrade the waqf land development and joint venture development through a partnership with developers to develop housing projects and business buildings. This implementation could support the small business entrepreneurs through the benefits of waqf lands and partnership contracts.

The third example is managing the waqf development in creating socio-economic development in society. Waqf organizations also can serve as business incubators for new ventures, nurturing and helping them to survive and prosper, and through the waqf mechanism they can provide finance or give loans to existing small businesses, and they build new capabilities and sustainable ventures. In addition, venture waqf opens a potential new direction in the transformative role that waqf can play for internalizing compassion in financial contracting and in developing an Islamic vision of entrepreneurship for achieving a waste-free halal market economy. In Johor, Majlis Agama Islam Johor (MAIJ), as a waqf trustee, also did some joint ventures in agriculture and farming with government agencies such as Federal Agricultural Marketing Authority (FAMA), and Malaysian Agricultural Research and Development Institute (MARDI). Omar et al. (2018) reported Johor Corporation and Bank Muamalat Malaysia Berhad are applied business corporations between financial institutions. Below is an example of the success of the corporate company in Malaysia JCorp and UDA Holdings.

Johor Corporation (JCorp)

The establishment of Corporate Waqf in 2006 by Johor Corporation (JCorp) has transformed waqf practice in Malaysia. For the first time, waqf assets in the form of shares of the company were issued and managed by a corporate body. It was first introduced by JCorp, a government-owned corporate business company (GLC), as a means of fulfilling Corporate Social Responsibility in contributing to the Muslim community in the country and is fully operated by its group subsidiary, Waqaf An-Nur Corporation Berhad (WANCorp). The company is a limited company established under JCorp's own guarantee and is responsible for distributing contributions to the community through the implementation of various welfare programs as a result of dividend profits from share units endowed by JCorp. WANCorp also acts as a maukuf alaihi on the waqf shares and other forms of securities of JCorp companies.

According to its founder, Tan Sri Muhammad Ali Hashim, the idea of creating corporate waqf derives from the notion of jihad business, pioneered by himself, with the main agenda being to improve the socio-economic wellbeing of Malay society in the country (Omar et al., 2018). Mohd Hanefah et al. (2011) explain in detail the structure of corporate waqf, which started with the pledge of shares amounting to RM200 million as waqf to WANCorp; a subsidiary of JCorp as a *nazir* (trustee). WANCorp manages and distributes waqf proceeds to the beneficiaries as stated in the waqf deed.

It is done through the waqf of share units owned by the group company comprising shares in listed and unlisted companies on Bursa Malaysia. Apart from waqf through group company share units, JCorp also waqf (endowed) several properties such as the Masjid An-Nur Plaza Kotaraya Johor Bharu site as the site of the Wakaf An-Nur Clinic. According to Tan Sri Muhammad Ali Hashim, the corporate waqf introduced by JCorp has its own waqf management method. It is the management method that distinguishes between JCorp's corporate waqf and waqf operated by waqf institutions in the country.

Tan Sri Muhammad Ali Hashim is the Former President and Chief Executive Officer of JCorp and the founder of WANCorp. He is the Deputy President, Malaysian Islamic Chamber of Commerce (DPIM), and Chairman of WANCorp. Among his services and roles during his tenure as President and Chief Executive Officer of JCorp is to introduce JCorp corporate waqf through waqf of company share units and create a network of An-Nur Waqf Hospitals and Clinics and An-Nur Dialysis Center based on the waqf concept.

The history of JCorp's corporate endowment began on July 8, 2005 through the waqf of 225,000 units of shares worth RM260,568 (Net Asset Value) in Tiram Travel Sdn. Bhd. (TTSB). TTSB is a subsidiary of the JCorp group which is not listed on Bursa Malaysia. Seeing the success of this initial waqf, on August 3, 2006 JCorp made another waqf by endowing a number of units of shares in three group subsidiaries listed on Bursa Malaysia – Kulim (Malaysia) Berhad, KPJ Healthcare Berhad, and Johor Land Berhad (Borham and Mahamood, 2013). Since then, the term 'corporate waqf' began to be widely used given its position as a corporate business company directly involved in waqf activities.

The term 'corporate waqf' is also often used by JCorp itself, especially in a series of campaigns and descriptions of corporate waqf as one of the company's welfare activities in fulfilling Corporate Social Responsibility or corporate social responsibility to society. On 10 October 10, 2007, JCorp endowed (waqf) a total of 75,000 share units (worth RM7,500) in the company Capaian Aspirasi Sdn. Bhd. While on 20 December 2007, JCorp endowed (waqf) a total of 50,325,000 share units (worth RM50 million) in the company TPM Management Sdn. Bhd.. Meanwhile, on December 20, 2007, JCorp endowed (waqf) a total of 50,325,000 units of shares (worth RM50 million) in TPM Management Sdn. Bhd. (Borham and Mahamood, 2013).

On December 4, 2009, a Memorandum of Understanding (MoU) was signed between JCorp and MAIJ as the sole trustee of waqf in the state. This agreement came into force on July 11, 2005, and has major implications for the future of JCorp as a corporate body in the country where MAIJ has agreed to appoint WANCorp as a Special Inspector whose role is to carry out powers and duties under Wakaf Rules 1983 under the Islamic Religious Administration Enactment, State of Johor 2003. This agreement has also given permission to JCorp to continue to endow (waqf) its company shares in accordance with the corporate endowment method (Borham and Mahamood, 2013). Indirectly, this agreement has given legal recognition or legitimacy to the corporate endowment institution through the establishment of WANCorp. In addition, this agreement is a recognition to WANCorp to grow into the first Waqf institution-level corporate body in Malaysia.

On June 29, 2009, WANCorp used the istibdal method of endowed Johor Land Berhad share units, as the company had been removed from a company listed on Bursa Malaysia. The replacement was done with a share unit in Al-'Aqar KPJ REIT, another subsidiary of JCorp listed on Bursa Malaysia. The total number of Al-'Aqar KPJ REIT shares endowed is 12.62 million units worth RM13 million, where the total value of shares replaced is equal to the value of Johor Land Berhad shares which is 4.32 million units of shares worth RM13 million previously endowed. As of December 2010, the total net asset value of endowed shares has increased to RM300.59 million from RM282.89 million in 2009. This includes the value of shares in listed and unlisted companies on Bursa Malaysia.

In general, JCorp's corporate endowment has made a significant contribution to the Muslim community in the country. As the party responsible for distributing the dividend profit from the share units, WANCorp will distribute it based on the waqf argument where 70 per cent is handed over to JCorp as Reinvestment and Human Development, 25 per cent to WANCorp for general welfare benefits, and 5 per cent is handed over to MAIJ (Borham and Mahamood, 2013). Since the endowment was done until December 2010, the total general welfare benefits received by WANCorp amounted to RM3,673,219.70.

Through the distribution of general welfare benefits, it is used to fund three main programs, which are corporate social responsibility programs, namely welfare and charity, human development, educational and entrepreneurial capital, as well as special projects. Among these are operating health services in 13 networks of Waqaf An-Nur Clinics (KWAN) and Dialysis Centers in four clinics and a waqf hospital managed by KPJ Healthcare Bhd. Since its inception, until December 2010, a total of 652,435 patients have received treatment throughout the KWAN network and endowment hospitals. Of these, a total of 612,844 people, or 93.9 per cent were Muslim patients and 39,591 people or 6.1 per cent were non-Muslim patients, while a total of 255 kidney patients were Muslim patients and received hemodialysis services with a machine capacity of 51 pieces.

The Waqaf An-Nur Clinic network is available at Waqaf An-Nur Hospital Pasir Gudang, Waqaf An-Nur Kotaraya Clinic, Waqaf An-Nur Clinic Batu Pahat, Waqaf An-Nur Senawang Clinic, Waqaf An-Nur Clinic Sungai Buloh, Selangor, Waqaf Clinic An-Nur Muar, Klinik Waqaf An-Nur Kluang, Klinik

Waqaf An-Nur Ijok, Kuala Selangor, Klinik Waqaf An-Nur Kuching, Sarawak, Klinik Waqaf An-Nur Samariang, Sarawak, Klinik Waqaf An-Nur Bukit Indah, Ampang, Waqaf An-Nur Larkin Sentral Clinic and the latest clinic is in Waqaf An-Nur Manjoi Clinic, Perak. Meanwhile, the Dialysis Centers are available at Waqaf An-Nur Pasir Gudang Hospital, KWAN Kotaraya Dialysis Center, KWAN Batu Pahat Dialysis Center, KWAN Senawang Dialysis Center, and KWAN Sarawak Dialysis Center. Borham and Mahamood (2013) report that WANCorp also plans to open a Kinik Wakaf An-Nur in Kelantan. Patients will be charged RM5 for each treatment including medication. For hemodialysis treatment, patients will be charged RM90 for each treatment. The balance of the actual cost will be borne by the Waqaf An-Nur Fund. The health services program is a program conducted under the management of KPJ Healthcare Berhad.

In addition, general welfare benefits are also used to fund the management of seven mosques, two religious schools, and the development of waqf land for the Darul Hanan Orphan Welfare Home. The mosques are An-Nur Kotaraya Mosque, Jamek Pasir Gudang Mosque, Taman Cendana Mosque, An-Nur Pasir Gudang Mosque, Jamek Ladang Ulu Tiram Mosque, Sibu Island Mosque and An-Nur Larkin Sentral Mosque. Meanwhile, the schools involved are Ladang Pasir Panjang Religious School and Sungai Papan Religious School. WANCorp also conducts activities and monitoring at ten mosques, three Friday small mosques, and 22 small mosques built in the plantation areas under the management of Kulim (Malaysia) Berhad. Currently, there are over 15,000 parishioners under the network of mosques managed by WANCorp with a total workforce of 17 people consisting of nine Imams and eight muezzins (Borham and Mahamood, 2013).

Through the education and entrepreneurship capital program, WANCorp has channeled contributions in the form of educational assistance to selected educational institutions such as the Johor Institute of Islamic Studies and Arabic Language (MARSAH), International Islamic University Malaysia (IIUM) student fund, State Integrated Religious Primary School, Johor (SRAB), braille al-Quran printing, and donations to local and foreign students. As for the entrepreneurship program, WANCorp has implemented a welfare loan program (Qard al-Hasan) known as Waqaf Dana Niaga (WDN). The program was first launched on May 5, 2007 is a capital to run a business especially for entrepreneurs involved in various businesses and the Ayamas Smart-Corner Entrepreneur Program (Borham and Mahamood, 2013). The Bistari-Sudut Ayamas Entrepreneur Program is a project jointly managed by KFC Marketing Sdn. Bhd. (KFCM). As of December 2009, the program has benefited 122 participants with loans amounting to RM247,750.00. Of the total, 92 recipients, or 75 per cent were women with 39 of them being participants in the Ayamas Smart-Corner Entrepreneur Program, and 31 people or

25 per cent were male. A monitoring unit called Ikhwan Muamalat has been established to establish good relations and provide business-related advisory services between participants and the management of Wakaf Dana Niaga (Borham and Mahamood, 2013).

WANCorp also undertook a special project by establishing the Waqf Brigade on June 28, 2007, officially launched on August 9, 2009 (Borham and Mahamood, 2013). The Waqf Brigade is a voluntary organization that plays a role in carrying out humanitarian aid missions and providing humanitarian assistance in the event of natural disasters to alleviate the burden of victims, help restore normal life after disasters and conduct humanitarian aid efforts based on the expertise and capabilities of the JCorp Group. In addition, a special project, namely the Imam Bukhari theater, was held in 2010 with an expenditure cost of 660,022.50 (Borham and Mahamood, 2013).

In addition, WANCorp also offers *mutawwif* services to accompany pilgrims for *Hajj* and *Umrah* through Tiram Travel Sdn.Bhd (TTSB). The *Mutawwif* service provided by TTSB is seen as a catalyst to the increase in the number of pilgrims. Looking at these developments, WANCorp has taken a proactive step by further strengthening the Mutawwif services offered by organizing *Mutawwif* Accreditation courses where accredited Mutawwifs have the opportunity to serve as *Mutawwif Umrah* and *Hajj* of TTSB companies. This Mutawwif service is also open to any travel company interested in using WANCorp's Mutawwif services. The program was implemented in 2006 until February 2010, and a total of six courses were conducted in which the number of participants who attended the course was 162 people (Borham and Mahamood, 2013).

UDA Holdings

The Urban Development Authority (UDA) was established by the government of Malaysia on November 12, 1971, to advance the nation's planned urban development for both commercial and residential purposes. UDA was incorporated on September 12, 1996, as UDA Holdings Sdn. Bhd., and later changed to UDA Holdings Berhad, effective July 14, 1999. Today, it is a GLC that is fully owned by the Ministry of Finance Incorporated (MoF Inc.) and is overseen by the Ministry of Entrepreneurial Development (MED) (UDA Holdings Berhad, 2021).

According to Ismail et al. (2016), one significant and successfully implemented Cross-Sector Partnership (CSP) in Waqf land development is the Wakaf Seetee Aishah (WSA) land in Pulau Pinang. The WSA land is a 9.86 acres of paddy field which was donated by Seetee Aishah Bt. Haji Mahmood on September 30, 1901.

During the land ownership surrender, Seetee Aishah requested the benefit from the WSA land should be used:

- to hold a memorial ceremony once during Ramadhan and pay a RM3 token to each participant for that event;
- to pay and supply the kerosene for all Mosques that located in Permatang Pauh during Ramadhan every year;
- sending money to Mecca and for *Umrah* purposes;
- the remaining balance needs to be used for any mosque maintenance in Permatang Pauh or sending money to Mecca in the name of Waqf or any philanthropic activity. Half of the remaining will be for the benefit of the ancestors (Saedah and Family).

In this joint venture, between UDA (developer), the capital provided by the MAINPP was the leased land while UDA contributed their expertise and funding. As a result, nine triple-storey shop units and 76 double-storey houses have been developed. The houses were sold by UDA at a range of prices between RM250,000 to RM400,000 each. MAINPP as one of the players in this CSP benefited from all the triple-storey shop lots (approximately RM10 million worth) plus 30 per cent of the profit from the net sales (after deducting the development cost) of the double-storey houses. Technically, the house has been sold (in terms of manfaah) to the buyer for 99 years on a leasehold basis as form 15 A was used; the ownership of the houses and the land will be returned to MAINPP at the end of the leased term.

This innovative development shifted the perceptions that waqf is just a religious product. It has proven waqf able to produce and generate income as well as filled the complexity of modern life. At the same time, Ismail, Salim and Hanafiah (2015) suggested that the issue of waqf land can be managed by strengthening and reforming waqf administration, registering all waqf land, improving the existing rental system, and offering tax relief to waqif.

THE WAQF STRATEGIES IN THE 11TH AND 12TH MALAYSIA PLANS

The intensity of the Malaysian government to strengthen waqf development is conveyed through the Malaysia Plan. The Malaysian Prime Minister announced in the 11th Malaysia Plan where waqf is giving priority/attention in four strategies, and the mid-term review of the 11th Malaysia Plan. For the 12th Malaysia plan, the National Waqf Master Plan is developed as a blueprint to achieve the targets. Below are the details of the 11th and 12th Malaysia Plans.

11th Malaysia Plan

In the 11th Malaysia Plan, 2016–2020 (2015), waqf is targeted in four strategies. First, waqf is stressed in Strategy E2 to increase Bumiputera's effective control and sustainable corporate ownership. In this strategy, waqf investment funds are created via crowdfunding to invest in profitable and high-potential companies. Second, as mentioned in Strategy E3 – Enlarging the Share of Bumiputera Wealth Ownership, collaboration with Yayasan Wakaf Malaysia (YWM), State Islamic Religious Council (SIRCs), and other Bumiputera-based institutions.

This collaboration enables Bumiputera institutions to purchase unsold Bumiputera lots. The institutions will own the property and receive rental income until the property is purchased by Bumiputera individuals. Third is under Strategy E4 – Empowering Bumiputera Economic Community. In this strategy, waqf funds and other Islamic banking are urged to create Bumiputera entrepreneurs in the strategic subsector. For instance, the halal industry. Fourth, strategy B2 is strengthening planning and implementation for better management of public housing. To improve the planning and development of affordable housing, an integrated database accessible to all relevant stakeholders will be established to ensure housing supply matches demand according to the locality, price, and target groups. Additionally, a land bank will be established for the development of affordable housing, particularly in urban areas. Collaboration between the National Housing Department and state Islamic religious councils could be leveraged to unlock potential waqf and baitulmal land.

Mid-term Review of the 11th Malaysia Plan

In the mid-term review of the 11th Malaysia Plan 2016–2020 (2018), five strategies are listed. First, Strategy A2 – Enhancing Bumiputera Economic Community (BEC), to increase wealth ownership. JAWHAR will formulate a comprehensive framework to develop potential waqf land through collaboration with Yayasan Wakaf Malaysia, SIRCs, and the state government. The comprehensive framework includes the management of cash waqf through crowdfunding, waqf certificate, and Sukuk. One of the strategies includes issuing waqf certificates specifically to increase community participation in waqf. Sukuk will be reviewed to facilitate fundraising on waqf land.

Second is Strategy B1 – Increasing Purchasing Power for All by providing more avenues offering affordable and competitive prices of goods and services. Cooperatives and waqf entities will offer affordable services in primary healthcare, pharmacies, and hotels. This is to improve market efficiency while reducing the community burden.

Strategy B2 is to provide quality and affordable housing by strengthening the housing waqf and *baitulmal*.

Fourth is in Strategy B3; that is, by enhancing the healthcare delivery system by optimizing financial resources healthcare through international fund and waqf. This has been proven by the collaboration with Ministry of Health (MoH) and SIRCs in providing Pusat Pembedahan Katarak MAIWP in Hospital Selayang and Pusat Bersalin Berisiko Rendah MAIWP in Hospital Putrajaya. The services are targeted at poor, low- and middle-income groups. Table 5.2 simplifies the Malaysia waqf strategies and aims in the 11th Malaysia Plan and the Mid-term Review of the 11th Malaysia Plan.

Strategy D2 is promoting the contributions of society and industry. This strategy highlights strengthening community support for education as an expanding public-private collaboration. The strategy is (i) by reaching out to industry alumni to leverage endowments for research and (ii) through the University Transformation Program (UniTP).

Next, the Mid-term 11th Malaysia Plan reported the 77 units of the medium–low-cost apartments (1,000 square feet) constructed on waqf land in Sungai Nibong, Pulau Pinang; 458 public affordable houses built on waqf land through smart partnership between Jabatan *Wakaf, Zakat dan Haji* and other institutions such as SIRCs, Yayasan Waqaf Malaysia, Lembaga Tabung Haji, private developers, and financial institutions.

The 12th Malaysia Plan: Waqf-Related Strategies

The 12th Malaysia Plan 2021–2025 consists of 13 chapters with three themes. Theme 1: Resetting the Economy; Theme 2: Strengthening Security, Wellbeing, and Inclusivity; and Theme 3: Advancing Sustainability (Economic Planning Unit, 2021). Specific focus will be given to the hardcore poor and poor in the bottom 10 per cent household income decile group (B1). This plan, with the objective of 'A Prosperous, Inclusive, Sustainable Malaysia', encompasses the first half of the Wawasan Kemakmuran Bersama 2030 (WKB 2030).

WKB 2030 was announced by former Prime Minister, Tan Sri Mahiaddin Yassin, in 2019. WKB 2030 aims to provide an enhanced standard of living for all by 2030 with three objectives, which are attaining development for all, addressing wealth and income disparities as well as making Malaysia a united, prosperous and dignified nation.

Malaysia's development path over the next 10 years will be guided by the WKB 2030, which aims to transform Malaysia into a united, prosperous, and dignified nation. The objective of the 12th Malaysia Plan is to achieve a prosperous, inclusive, and sustainable Malaysia, in line with the WKB 2030 and the 2030 Agenda. Sustainable economic growth will be accompanied by fair, equitable, and inclusive economic distribution across all income

Table 5.2   *Malaysia waqf strategies and aims in the 11th Malaysia Plan*
                     and the Mid-term Review of the 11th Malaysia Plan

Malaysia Plan	Strategy	Aim
11th Malaysia Plan (2015-2020)	Strategy E2: Increasing Bumiputera effective control and sustainable corporate ownership	Waqf investment funds are created via crowd funding to invest in profitable and high potential companies.
	Strategy E3: Enlarging the share of Bumiputera wealth ownership.	Collaboration with Yayasan Wakaf Malaysia (YWM), State Islamic Religious Council (SIRC) and other Bumiputera-based institutions. Enable Bumiputera institutions to purchase unsold Bumiputera lots in new property.
	Strategy E4: Empowering Bumiputera Economic Community	Waqf fund and other Islamic banking are urged to create Bumiputera entrepreneurs in strategic subsectors (e.g. halal industry)
	Strategy B2: Strengthening planning and implementation for better management of public housing.	Integrated database accessible to all relevant stakeholders will be established to ensure housing supply matches demand according to locality, price, and target groups. A land bank will be established for the development of affordable housing, particularly in urban areas. Collaboration between the National Housing Department and state Islamic religious councils could be leveraged to unlock potential waqf and baitulmal land.
Mid-term Review of the 11th Malaysia Plan (2016–2020)	Strategy A2: Enhancing Bumiputera Economic Community (BEC) to increase wealth ownership.	JAWHAR will formulate a comprehensive framework to develop potential waqf land through collaboration with Yayasan Wakaf Malaysia, SIRC and state government.
	Strategy B1: Increasing purchasing power for all	Cooperatives and waqf entities will offer affordable services in primary healthcare, pharmacies and hotels.
	Strategy B2: Providing quality and affordable housing	By strengthening the housing waqf and baitulmal.

Malaysia Plan	Strategy	Aim
	Strategy B3: Enhancing the healthcare delivery system	By optimizing financial resources healthcare through international funds and waqf.
	Strategy D2: Promoting contributions of society and industry.	Strengthening community support for education, expanding public–private collaboration: i. by reaching out to industry alumni to leverage endowments for research ii. through University Transformation Program (UniTP).

groups, ethnicities, and regions to provide a decent standard of living for all Malaysians. In addition, the 12th Malaysia Plan encompasses strategies and initiatives that safeguard national security and sovereignty, which are vital for sustainable socio-economic development.

The 12th Malaysia Plan is aligned to the 2030 Agenda, representing Malaysia's commitment to implementing the 17 SDGs. There are six chapters, which focus on waqf development. Each of the chapters in the 12th Malaysia Plan elaborates according to (i) introduction of the chapter in the Malaysia Plan's report; (ii) performance on the 11th Malaysia Plan; (iii) issues and challenges; and (iv) way forward (which refers to 12th Malaysia Plan). Thus, the explanation below highlights the introduction of the chapter (as in the report) and the way forward. The six chapters in the 12th Malaysia Plan are as in Table 5.3.

Restoring growth momentum
The focus of Chapter 2 in the 12th Malaysia Plan is on boosting productivity, mainly through accelerating technology adoption, expanding market exports, strengthening the effectiveness of the financial intermediation ecosystem, enhancing the role of industrial estates as well as improving governance and

Table 5.3   The six chapters mentioning waqf in the 12th Malaysia Plan

	Chapter	Title of the chapter in the 12th Malaysia Plan
1	Chapter 2	Restoring Growth Momentum
2	Chapter 3	Propelling growth of strategic and high impact Industries as well as micro, small and medium enterprises
3	Chapter 4	Enhancing defense, security, wellbeing, and unity
4	Chapter 5	Addressing poverty and building an inclusive society
5	Chapter 10	Developing future talents
6	Chapter 11	Boosting digitalization and advanced technology

policy. In this chapter, Waqf is discussed in two targets: Priority Area C and Priority Area E.

Priority Area C targets promoting a sustainable and Inclusive Financial System. In priority Area C, the focus for modernizing the waqf instrument is on strategy C3: Promoting Islamic financing and enhancing sustainable financial services.

Promoting the Islamic Finance Agenda

Malaysia aims to sustain its position as a leading international Islamic financial center. This includes exploring the usage of social finance instruments through blending endowment (waqf), donation (*sadaqah*), and alms-giving (*zakat*), to further unlock and more effectively mobilize resources towards the provision of financing and financial protection to low-income communities. In this regard, measures will be undertaken to develop more innovative market-based mechanisms and products, leveraging on Islamic Fintech, to better serve the needs of a wider financial market and the economy at large.

Enhancing Sustainable Financial Services

In enhancing Sustainable Financial Services, Islamic financial institutions are primed to advance the sustainability agenda, through initiatives such as the value-based intermediation (VBI) framework. Through VBI, Islamic finance will bring various stakeholders together to advance the sustainability agenda. VBI also encourages Islamic financial institutions to assess how they create value and impact, particularly in response to changing economic, social, and environmental conditions. This will support socio-economic development in line with Malaysia's long-term agenda of economic growth and shared prosperity for all. In addition, efforts to develop a facilitative Sustainable and Responsible Investment (SRI) ecosystem under the SRI Roadmap will also be intensified. Islamic finance will also be leveraged to further advance SRI solutions. This will include broadening Islamic capital market products and services to further support social finance activities, such as waqf, for the greater good of society.

The priority Area E aims to improve the policy for waqf. It is mentioned in strategy E1. Strong governance accompanied by comprehensive policies and legislations that are responsive to changes will facilitate the economic sectors moving up the value chain and attracting high-quality investment. In strategy E1, the priority is encouraging sharing of data and resources. Availability of accurate and comprehensive data and information, as well as sufficient resources, is vital in providing better services to customers. Collaboration among private HEIs will be promoted in sharing resources, including facilities and equipment to improve the quality of teaching and learning. In addition, the private HEIs will be encouraged to explore alternative financing, including waqf and crowdfunding in ensuring the sustainability of the institutions.

In conclusion, the initiatives to modernize waqf roles in Chapter 2 – Restoring Growth Momentum can be understood through promoting a sustainable and Inclusive Financial System (priority C) and waqf policy (priority E). Through both priorities, the initiatives that the 12th Malaysia Plan proposes are, by developing more innovative market-based mechanisms and products, leveraging Islamic Fintech, broadening Islamic capital market products, and exploring alternative financing for HEIs.

Propelling growth of strategic and high impact industries as well as micro, small and medium enterprises
In Chapter 3 of the 12th Malaysia Plan, the initiatives will be undertaken to enhance the contribution of strategic and high-impact industries in regenerating economic growth. The waqf roles are in Strategy A6 in priority area A. Priority Area A focuses on accelerating the Development of Strategic and High Impact Industries. One of the industries is fostering the competitiveness of the halal industry. The industries are prioritized based on their ability to harness advanced technologies and niche capabilities, as well as their significant multiplier effects. The implementation of these strategies is expected to increase the contribution of the industries to Gross Domestic Product (GDP) growth, create high-paying jobs and boost export earnings.

The global halal landscape is rapidly changing, as rising demand has resulted in the entrance of many new global players that offer halal products and services. Hence, the halal industry development will be strengthened to produce competitive domestic halal industry players in capturing a bigger global halal market share. Measures will be undertaken to enhance the capacity and capability of the halal industry by uplifting the development of halal talent, establishing halal professional recognition, accelerating industry development including Bumiputera participation, increasing product competitiveness, and positioning Malaysia as a global halal hub. These measures are expected to contribute to the growth of the halal industry, increasing its share of GDP to 8.1 per cent and generating RM56 billion export revenue in 2025.

Accelerating halal industry development to enhance competitiveness
The halal industry will be further developed by leveraging domestic strength, including by increasing the participation of Bumiputera companies through the implementation of the Halal Industry Master Plan 2030 (HIMP 2030). The Master Plan aims to enhance halal industry development by creating a larger talent pool, improving integrated infrastructure, and accelerating the production of high value-added products and services to better capture the global halal market opportunities. Collaboration and co-investment between

local and international businesses will be encouraged to commercialize R&D output to enhance the competitiveness and resilience of the industry. Under this initiative, local halal entrepreneurs will be encouraged to venture into the production of high value-added products, such as halal ingredients, pharmaceuticals, cosmetics, and medical devices.

The role of SMEs will be enhanced to be a key driver for the development of the halal industry. High-performing SMEs will be groomed as home-grown halal local champions. This will involve upscaling production capacity and product quality as well as promoting local brands to be on par with global brands in improving access to the international market. In addition, the capacity and capability of local companies will be strengthened to facilitate participation in the supply chain of MNCs. The Malaysia Halal Analysis Centre (MyHAC) will be enhanced to improve its function in conducting analysis and providing scientific evidence for halal authentication and traceability. The tracking and monitoring mechanisms for halal integrity along the supply chain will be improved to be more transparent and further boost consumer confidence. Inclusive participation, particularly involving Bumiputera companies in the halal supply chain will be further promoted through the improvement of existing programs and the creation of new programs to facilitate the expansion of high-value products. Halal innovation-focused business incubator programs will also be implemented to grow local companies and connect with other business incubators globally for better networking, acceptance, and recognition. A dedicated fund for halal exporters will be established to support the formation of consortiums, improve branding and promote business matching with global partners to capture a larger share of the halal market. In addition, fundraising activities through waqf and equity crowdfunding will be conducted to support halal business start-ups.

Chapter 3 – Propelling Growth of Strategic and High impact Industries as well as Micro, Small and Medium Enterprises – concludes with the waqf roles fostering the competitiveness of an inclusive halal industry as mentioned in Strategy A6 in priority area A, by fundraising through waqf and equity crowdfunding supporting halal business start-ups.

Enhancing defense, security, wellbeing, and unity
In Chapter 4 of the 12th Malaysia Plan, the focus is on healthcare and housing aspects. First is Priority Area B, which is by Enhancing Healthcare Service Delivery, and second is Priority Area C, which is by Increasing the Supply of Quality Affordable Housing.

Priority Area B aims to improve the wellbeing of the rakyat, and more focus will be given to enhancing healthcare service delivery through revitalizing of the healthcare system and greater collaboration in the consolidation of resources. The healthcare system will be redesigned, while health financing and public awareness will be strengthened. Emerging technologies will be leveraged to support the initiatives for better provision of healthcare services. The implementation of these measures will contribute to ensuring healthy lives and promoting the wellbeing of the rakyat. A national health endowment fund, particularly from waqf will be introduced as a measure to diversify sources of funding and create alternative financing for healthcare. The strategy has been mentioned in B2 in priority area B, which is to strengthen the health financing and public awareness to ensure sustainable healthcare financing and to strengthen health protection coverage for targeted groups.

In addition, health literacy and awareness among the public will be enhanced through the implementation of various programs at all levels. The implementation of these initiatives is expected to facilitate the delivery of quality healthcare services. It also targets reducing government burden and gradually providing sustainable quality healthcare services. The Malaysia National Health Accounts report will be strengthened by incorporating a more detailed analysis of public health expenditure as a tool to identify cost drivers within the health system. Current healthcare charges will be reviewed so that higher-income patients will be required to pay higher charges. Subsidies for healthcare services will be streamlined based on a means test. Several approaches, including public–private partnership, rent-to-own, leasing, and sharing of facilities will be explored in reducing dependency on Government allocations.

Priority Area C aims to increase the Supply of Quality Affordable Housing. Emphasis will be given to improving access to affordable housing by enhancing affordable housing governance and ensuring inclusive housing development. These strategies are in line with WKB 2030 and the 2030 Agenda that aims to provide access to adequate, safe, and affordable housing for all. Through strategy C1 in priority C, the 12th Malaysia Plan aims to provide better access to affordable housing. This will be achieved by ensuring the provision of affordable housing for target groups, increasing access to financing, and managing housing construction costs to facilitate homeownership. Efforts will continue to be undertaken to capitalize on government-owned and waqf land to enable higher ownership of affordable housing for selected target groups.

As a conclusion for Chapter 4 – Enhancing Defense, Security, Wellbeing and Unity, the 12th Malaysia Plan aims at two categories: enhancing healthcare service (Priority Area B) and supplying affordable housing in Priority Area C. In priority area B, the waqf fund will be introduced as a national health endowment fund to diversify sources of funding and create alternative financing for healthcare. In priority C, the aim is to modernize the use of waqf land for the selected target group in developing affordable housing.

Addressing poverty and building an inclusive society

In Chapter 5 of the 12th Malaysia Plan, the initiatives addressing poverty and inclusivity are consistent with the principle of leaving no one behind, achieving a decent standard of living, and ensuring social justice. This strategy is an integral part of WKB 2030, which supports the commitment of Malaysia to be a developed and prosperous nation, with fair and equitable wealth distribution across income groups, ethnicities, and supply chains. This is also in line with the 2030 Agenda. In this regard, concerted efforts will be undertaken in further reducing hardcore poverty incidence, achieving equitability for all, while addressing current and future challenges, including the impact of the COVID-19 pandemic.

These initiatives are expected to raise the income and standard of living of the poor households regardless of ethnicity, B40, and M40. The issues and challenges in waqf are when the development of Malay Reserve Land (MRL) and waqf land are still limited due to lack of financial capabilities and governance issues. The total size of MRL decreased from 5.04 million hectares in 2017 to 4.88 million hectares in 2019 because of difficulties in finding equivalent land for replacement. There are no comprehensive data on the total size of waqf land. The absence of a common regulatory framework to govern the MRL and waqf land leads to uncoordinated planning and development. Thus, strategy D6 mentions optimizing the MRL and waqf instruments.

Strategy D6 is strengthening the Development of Malay Reserve Land (MRL) and waqf Instruments to achieve an Equitable Outcome for Bumiputera. In this regard, state authorities are encouraged to develop MRL and waqf lands through collaborations with Federal agencies. An integrated master plan on the development of MRL, waqf land, and waqf instruments is formulated to provide a framework for socio-economic development at state and local levels. The role and scope of the Peninsular Malaysia Malay Reserve Data Management Steering Committee will be expanded to provide guidelines relating to land development and value creation. It is understood that a committee comprising representatives of federal and state governments will be set up to provide overall direction in planning, implementation, and monitoring of waqf land development. In addition, the possibility of expanding the concept of waqf as an instrument for broader socio-economic development will be explored. A waqf fund at the Federal level will be established to mobilize resources from individuals and corporate bodies to fund socio-economic activities. These initiatives will be implemented without compromising the status of the state Islamic religious councils as sole trustees of the waqf assets.

As a conclusion for Chapter 5 – Addressing Poverty and Building an Inclusive Society, the 12th Malaysia Plan aims at strengthening the Development of Malay Reserve Land (MRL) and waqf Instruments to achieve Strategy D6. Collaboration is needed between state authorities and federal agencies to develop MRL and waqf lands. A waqf fund at the Federal level will be established to mobilize resources from individuals and corporate bodies to fund socio-economic activities.

Developing future talents

In Chapter 10, the aim is to re-align the labor market for inclusive and sustainable growth as well as to develop future-ready talents. The focus is to increase job opportunities for Malaysians, achieve equitable compensation of employees (CE), improve labor participation, and strengthen labor market support. Strategies to produce future-ready talents include improving the quality of academic and training programs, ensuring equitable learning outcomes, leveraging emerging technologies, and strengthening the governance. In chapter 10, the role of waqf is mentioned in Priority B – Developing Future-ready Talent in strategy B2 – which discussed the roles of waqf instruments.

Waqf instruments are mentioned in priority area B, which focuses on developing Future-ready Talent. It is imperative to meet the changing skills required by industry and to embrace the rapid technology change. Emphasis will be given to raise the quality of education and training programs, strengthen governance, leverage emerging technology, ensure equitable learning outcomes and address overlap TVET governance. In strategy B2, waqf instruments are more on Strengthening Governance. Education governance will be strengthened to support the development of future-ready talent. This will include enhancing governance and coordination of the schooling system as well as fostering effective governance and providing greater financial independence to HEIs. These initiatives will enhance the delivery of education and training by schools, HEIs and Technical and Vocational Education and Training (TVET) institutions. Strategy B2 has two targets: (i) Enhancing Governance and Coordination of the School System, and (ii) Fostering Effective Governance and Greater Financial Independence of HEIs. Thus, for Waqf instruments, Guidelines on Good Practices (GGP) on international accreditation will be developed as an initiative to improve quality and strengthen niche programs.

This initiative will ensure programs offered are up-to-date, industry-relevant, in line with international best practices, and accredited by international organizations. The financial sustainability of HEIs will be strengthened. These will include reviewing fees and prioritizing R&D activities. Existing facilities in HEIs, including teaching hospitals, will be utilized for income-generating services. HEIs will also be encouraged to expand alternative financial pathways. This will include refining and facilitating the management of funds sourced from waqf, endowment, donations, and crowdfunding. For this purpose, a comprehensive policy and GGP on a financing model will be formulated and a mechanism to monitor income-generating activities and programs will be developed. In addition, HEIs will be urged to develop a new financing model to source contributions from the industry, multinational companies (MNCs), SMEs, financial institutions, and the community. The MyWakalah initiative will be further enhanced as an alternative.

As a conclusion for Chapter 10 – Developing Future Talents, the 12th Malaysia Plan is aimed at priority area B, which focuses on developing Future-ready Talents. Strategy B2 includes enhancing governance and coordination of the schooling system as well as fostering effective governance and providing greater financial independence to HEIs. Thus, for waqf instruments, GGP on international accreditation will be developed as an initiative to improve quality.

Boosting Digitalization and Advanced Technology

In Chapter 11, during the 12th Plan, the initiatives to boost digitalization and advanced technology adoption are emphasized. The focus is on advancing the digital economy, mainstreaming digitalization for inclusive development, accelerating research, development, commercialization and innovation (R&D&C&I) as well as capitalizing on the potential of emerging technologies. The initiatives are expected to enhance national competitiveness and resilience, thus preparing Malaysia to be a high technology-based economy. Thus, priority area C in strategy C1 is aimed at accelerating R&D&C&I.

In priority area C, R&D&C&I plays a crucial role in fostering innovation and accelerating socio-economic development towards ensuring a better quality of life. The 12th Malaysia Plan will continue to place a high priority on developing and leveraging science, technology, and innovation (STI) by strengthening R&D&C&I's capacity and capability. It will also nurture quality STI talents to improve R&D&C&I's outcomes.

The roles of waqf in Strategy C1 focus on strengthening the funding for research, development, commercialization, and innovation. The newly formed Research Management Unit (RMU), under the Economic Planning Unit of the Prime Minister's Department, coordinates and harmonizes the funding mechanisms for all R&D&C&I activities in ensuring these activities are in line with national priorities. The RMU ensures at least 50 percent of the total R&D expenditure in the 12th Malaysia Plan is for experimental development research with high commercialization potential. Measures will be undertaken to increase access to alternative financing including through venture capital and international funding. In addition, an endowment fund will be established to source funds from industry, matching grants, crowdfunding, and waqf, for STI-related R&D activities. The implementation of these initiatives is expected to increase the percentage of Gross Expenditure on R&D (GERD) to GDP to 2.5 per cent by 2025.

Table 5.4   *Strategies to modernize waqf instrument in the 12th Malaysia Plan*

Chapter	Priority areas	Strategies	Targets
2 – Restoring Growth Momentum	C: Promoting a sustainable and Inclusive Financial System E: Improving governance and policy	C3: promoting a sustainable and inclusive financial system E1: strengthening coordination and collaboration	• To develop more innovative market- based mechanisms and products • To leverage Islamic Fintech • To broaden Islamic capital market products • To explore alternative financing for Higher Education Institutions
3 – Propelling Growth of Strategic and High Impact Industries as well as SMEs	A: Competitiveness of Inclusive Halal Industry	Strategy A6: fundraising through Waqf and equity crowdfunding	• To support halal business start-ups
4 – Enhancing Defense, Security, Wellbeing and Unity	B: Enhancing healthcare service C: Supply affordable housing		• Waqf fund will be introduced as a national health endowment fund and create alternative financing for healthcare • Waqf land for selected target group in developing affordable housing
5 – Addressing Poverty and Building an Inclusive Society	D: strengthening the Development of Malay Reserve Land (MRL) and Waqf Instruments	Strategy D6: Collaboration is needed between state authorities and federal agencies to develop MRL and Waqf lands	• Waqf fund at the Federal level will be established
10 – Developing Future Talent	B: Developing Future-Ready Talent	Strategy B2: enhancing governance and coordination of the schooling system and providing greater financial independence to HEI	• For waqf instruments, Guidelines on Good Practices (GGP) on international accreditation will be developed as an initiative to improve quality
11 – Boosting digitalization and advanced technology	C: Accelerating Research, Development, Commercialization and Innovation		• Waqf fund will be established to source funds from industry, matching grants, crowdfunding and Waqf, for STI-related R&D activities

As a conclusion for Chapter 11 – Boosting Digitalization and Advanced Technology, the 12th Malaysia Plan aims, through priority area C, at accelerating Research, Development, Commercialization, and Innovation. The endowment fund will be established to source funds from industry, matching grants, crowdfunding, and waqf, for STI-related R&D activities. Table 5.4 summarizes the details.

In conclusion, through the 11th Malaysia plan, mid-term review 11 Malaysia Plan, and 12th Malaysia Plan, Malaysia has vigorously improved the roles of waqf as social finance economic growth or as a third sector economy source. The National Waqf Masterplan (2021–2025), which is established to ensure a more efficient Waqf management and to maximize the waqf assets' mobility in the future is an accurate decision. Indeed, one of the most pressing issues in need of waqf support in today's world is science and technology.

Waqf in Malaysia is managed by Malaysia Waqf Foundation (MWF) under the JAWHAR in the Prime Minister's Department. The establishment is to monitor the effectiveness and efficiency of waqf, *zakat* (alms-giving), and *hajj* administration in all 13 states in Malaysia. To date, MWF has offered two types of products: the cash waqf scheme and the building waqf certificate. The structure of waqf governance is formed based on the participation from the government (establishment of Malaysia Waqf Foundation in JAWHAR) and AIBIM. Currently, Malaysia is practicing four types of contemporary waqf, namely cash waqf, waqf asset, Sukuk, and corporate waqf.

Waqf development has been prioritized, especially in the 11th Malaysia Plan, the mid-term review of the 11th Malaysia Plan, and in the 12th Malaysia plan. The 11th Malaysia Plan focused on waqf funds through investment, economic community, and managing waqf land. In the mid-term review of the 11th Malaysia Plan, the waqf instrument continued to serve in developing waqf land with formulating a comprehensive framework, waqf services in healthcare, pharmacies and hotels, waqf housing, and in an education learning institution. In the 12th Malaysia Plan, the roles of waqf are expanded to promote a sustainable Islamic financial system, improve governance policy, the halal industry for SMEs, strengthen the development of Malay Reserve land, provide financial independence to Higher Learning Institution and invest in digitalization and advanced technology through waqf funds. In addition, the Malaysia Waqf Master Plan as a blueprint will be produced to solidify the waqf instrument as social finance.

6. Waqf for small and medium enterprises

This chapter highlights the waqf application for entrepreneurship activities, which focuses on small and medium enterprises (SMEs). Entrepreneurship can be translated into two categories which are small and medium, or a large-scale business owner. Both have contributed significantly to job creation, innovation and economic growth (Ku Hanani, 2021). The terms of entrepreneurship are different for corporation and SMEs but both have similar goals in waqf target. Therefore, in this section, the focus will be on the SMEs in the waqf application. This section highlights on how waqf can help SMEs to face challenges due to the COVID-19 pandemic as well as the possible solutions that can be taken by SMEs in relation to waqf application.

SMEs act as a catalyst for economic growth (Gamidullaeva et al., 2020). SMEs are the foundation of many economies across the world, accounting for 95 per cent of all businesses and 60 per cent of all occupations. SMEs are a significant part of most governments' development strategies, with SMEs accounting for 60 per cent of economies in developed nations and 99 per cent of firms in developing countries (Zulu-Chisanga et al., 2021). In Southeast Asia, SMEs dominate the business environment representing 97.2 per cent of all enterprises, 69.4 per cent of the national workforce, and 41.1 per cent of a country's gross domestic product (GDP) between 2010 and 2019. Although SMEs account for a large share of the economic activity, SMEs face various challenges in obtaining financing, and options for sources of funding are very limited from financial institutions (FIs), particularly in developing economies (Artini & Ni Luh Putu, 2020). It is also important to realize that finance is crucial to SMEs as it is not just a driver of a firm's growth that influences most of the other key challenges (Wasiuzzaman et al., 2020). Due to SMEs' nature, they potentially face moral hazards by being wrongly categorized by FIs which attempt to obtain credit to reduce their financial institution's risk of default. In Southeast Asia, the performance of SMEs' non-performing loans as a percentage of total SME bank loans was an average of 4.1 per cent during the same period, a 2.5 per cent decline at a compound annual rate, but higher than the overall bank average (2.0 per cent).

THE IMPORTANCE OF SMALL AND MEDIUM ENTERPRISES

Small and medium enterprises (SMEs) are important in most economies, especially in developing nations. The definitions of SMEs vary among countries. In Malaysia, SMEs can be identified based on two components: first, their sales turnover, and second, the number of their full-time employees. It varies across different sectors. Sales turnover in the manufacturing industry should not exceed RM50 million, with no more than 200 full-time employees. In contrast, sales turnover in the services and other industries should not exceed RM20 million, and full-time workers should not exceed 75 (SME Corporation Malaysia, 2021a). On the other hand, micro enterprises are categorized as firms with the sales turnover of less than RM300,000 or the number of employees of fewer than five for all sectors including manufacturing and services (SME Corporation Malaysia, 2021b).

Indonesia, on the other hand, refers to SMEs as firms with fewer than a hundred employees (Tambunan, 2008). According to the Law Number 20, 2008, small enterprises own assets worth Rp50 million to Rp 500 million and obtain between Rp 300 million to Rp 2.5 billion of revenue yearly. Medium enterprises own assets worth Rp 500 million to Rp 10 billion, and obtain between Rp 2.5 billion to Rp 50 billion of revenue per annum (Dipta, 2017). Micro enterprise is a term used to describe small companies founded and run by underprivileged people with the help of sponsoring organizations (Midgley, 2008). Indonesia's Law Number 20, 2008 also defines a microenterprise as an efficient business run individually or a corporate organization that meets the conditions for microenterprise as established in the Law; a business with maximum asset worth Rp50 million or maximum yearly revenue of Rp300 million (Tambunan, 2019).

To accommodate the expanding global workforce, The World Bank Group predicted that 600 million jobs will be required by 2030, making SMEs' growth a top priority for many governments throughout the world. However, SMEs are not exempted from facing challenges and obstacles in their businesses, such as difficulties coping with recession, barriers posed by global sourcing, low productivity, lack of organizational expertise, lack of funding and access to technology (Muhammad et al., 2009). Not only that, but SMEs are unlikely to be able to acquire bank loans as compared to large businesses, forcing them to depend on internal funds to run their enterprises (World Bank Group, 2022). Different countries respond using a variety of strategic tools and resources.

SMEs play a critical role in fulfilling the SDGs. SMEs have produced four out of every five available employments in developing economies, accounting for around 90 per cent of total formal sector employment. SMEs provide jobs, which boosts the economy and assists the poor and vulnerable, notably women and youth (Harris, 2018). They alleviate poverty, provide money, and have a favorable influence on household investments in education and healthcare, all of which are critical to achieving multiple SDGs.

According to a report by OECD in 2016, SMEs make up the majority business in the OECD 42 regions, acting as the primary source of employment accounting for over 70 per cent of all employment on average and are significant contributors to value creation, providing between 50 per cent and 60 per cent of total value added (OECD, 2016). It was also found that SMEs account for up to 45 per cent of total employment and 33 per cent of GDP in emerging economies. When informal firms are factored in, SMEs represent more than half of all employments and GDP in most countries, regardless of income level (Internal Finance Corporation, 2010).

The importance of SMEs in economic development has long been acknowledged from a global viewpoint, as they have historically been the major source of job/employment generation as well as economic expansion. The widespread belief continues to be that a thriving private sector, particularly SMEs, is critical to the achievement of sustainable and equitable economic development in a democratic society (Rahman et al., 2016). It was further found that despite the fact that many SMEs' products are purchased by middle- and high-income consumers, it is clear that SMEs' products are overwhelmingly simple consumer goods, such as clothing, furniture, and other articles and household items made of wood, bamboo, and rattan, leather products, including footwear, and various metal products (Tambunan, 2015). These items are designed to meet the demands of low-income or impoverished consumers in the area, which showed that SMEs are critical for ensuring that the disadvantaged have access to basic essentials.

Apart from that, it was discovered that SMEs are important in the attempts to attain environmental sustainability. Participation of SMEs in the shift to more environmentally friendly patterns of production and consumption is critical for developing green economic development. Despite the fact that small businesses have a lower individual environmental footprint than large corporations, their aggregate environmental impact can be greater than that of large corporations in some sectors. In order to be successful in the green transition, SMEs must reduce their environmental effects by attaining and moving beyond environmental compliance with existing norms and regulations in both manufacturing and services. This is especially important for SMEs in the manufacturing sector, which represents a significant portion of the world's resource consumption, air and water pollution, and waste creation (OECD, 2013).

SMEs are undeniably important in the economic growth of many countries, representing 90 per cent of businesses and more than 50 per cent employment worldwide. They are a significant source of entrepreneur's skills and innovation for most enterprises throughout the world. Therefore, the development of SMEs is considered important for every country globally.

In Indonesia, for example, SMEs make up over 90 per cent of all businesses across all industries, where agriculture accounts for the majority of these businesses, with trade, hotels and restaurants coming in second and manufacturing coming in third (Tambunan, 2008). According to Bank Indonesia in 2020, they aid in the development of micro, small and medium enterprises, emphasizing access to credit for SMEs as part of their mission. It was also discovered that SMEs contribute significantly to Indonesia's economic growth by generating gross domestic product and employing a significant workforce. In empowering their SMEs and further improving the ability and management competencies of human resources in the SME sector while encouraging innovation, Bank Indonesia has implemented several policies, such as:

1. Improving the monetary policy efficacy and policy mix of Bank Indonesia to attain Rupiah's stability.
2. Enhancing the synergy among Bank Indonesia's policy mix, fiscal policy, and structural reforms in order to control the budget deficit and catalyze long-term economic growth.
3. Establishing Bank Indonesia policy in collaboration with other stakeholders to aid the growth of the Islamic economy and finance.

This demonstrates that SMEs in Indonesia are recognized as key players in the economy and may act as a catalyst to achieve the economic prosperity by promoting inclusive and sustainable growth, offering quality employment, and reducing income disparities.

SMEs account for 99 per cent of current firms in Indonesia and create more than 60 per cent of national GDP (Sakudo, 2021). Even before the pandemic, the necessity of business digitization for SMEs was on the radar. The nation has announced programs such as the 2018 Making Indonesia 4.0 Roadmap, the 2019 E-Commerce Roadmap, and the 2020 Go Digital Vision, all of which emphasize assistance for strengthening SMEs' competitiveness in the digital economy. Collaborations between businesses and the government is also essential for SMEs to flourish. The official Gojek digital platform, for example, cooperates with a variety of stakeholders, including the government, to provide solutions that help SMEs progress to the next level through its initiative, #MelajuBersamaGojek. This program, according to Gojek co-CEO Andre Soelistyo, is an attempt by the Gojek ecosystem to make it easier for SMEs to integrate digitalization at every stage of their everyday company operations (*The Jakarta Post*, 2020). The importance of SMEs is further enhanced through digitalization.

SMEs are often regarded as the economy's backbone, accounting for 98.5 per cent of all company establishments in Malaysia (Safie, 2020). SMEs make up a significant portion of the economy and, consequently, contribute significantly to a country's growth. According to the Malaysian Department of Statistics, the contribution of SMEs to overall GDP grew to 38.9 per cent in 2019 from 38.3 per cent in 2018. However, the recent COVID-19 pandemic has had a huge impact on SMEs' growth, where GDP dropped by 7.3 per cent in 2020, which was worse than the 5.6 per cent and 4.6 per cent declines in Malaysia's GDP and non-SMEs GDP. Various efforts done in preventing the spread of COVID-19 have led to the downfall of all economic sectors, particularly SMEs (Ikram, 2021).

However, due to the pandemic, many SMEs are struggling to maintain their financial stability, especially with the COVID-19 pandemic sweeping across the globe. In addition, with Malaysia's Movement Control Order (MCO) in place, some SMEs are seeing close to a 50 per cent drop in income. The outbreak of the coronavirus has slowed the global economy and most companies are in a state of instability. Although the COVID-19 pandemic impacts everyone, those most adversely affected are workers who are paid on a daily basis, and SMEs (Mahendhiran, 2020). A survey by an online home services platform, Recommend.my, found that 68.9 per cent of local SMEs suffered more than a 50 per cent drop in business within one week of the MCO. The survey, which studied SMEs' sentiments one week prior to the lockdown and one week after, found that almost 100 per cent of local businesses had a negative outlook for the Malaysian economy for the rest of the year, with more than half having a negative outlook on their own businesses (Annuar, 2020). Therefore, the role of waqf is very significant in recovering the economic sector by giving opportunities to SMEs to survive.

The importance of SMEs is highlighted in terms of numbers where SMEs have successfully employed 7.25 million people in 2020, 0.9 per cent fewer, or 65,000 people, compared with the previous year (7.32 million) people. SMEs' employment fell more than Malaysian or national employment throughout the year, demonstrating that SMEs were particularly badly impacted by the COVID-19 health crisis. Prior to 2020, the average annual change in SME employment was 3.0 per cent, or around 200,000 people added per year (DOSM, 2021).

Therefore, it is said that SMEs are the major contributors to the country's economic growth and play a key role in molding the country's future (SME Corp, 2021a). SMEs, particularly microenterprises, have played a critical role in promoting development, employment, and income in Malaysia's economic progress. It is stated that SMEs have been acknowledged as important sources of growth and as the foundation for the country's rapid economic growth and development. The major cause for this was due to their overall numbers, sizes, and the various natures of their businesses.

WAQF AND ENTREPRENEURSHIP ACTIVITIES

This section will highlight findings from research, practices by many countries that can be adopted and adapted by waqf organizations and countries in order to help SMEs.

Cash waqf has been identified as an important element in SMEs' programs. Cash waqf benefits the SMEs in the following ways: first, the donor himself in the first place will be one of the beneficiaries of the waqf; second, cash waqf also creates a great opportunity for SMEs by getting financial reward and profit which can be channeled to their needs according to their terms during the establishment of the cash waqf; third, it increases the accumulation of liquidity and capital in the industry and creates more business opportunities; fourth, it improves the market by increasing more business activities; and fifth, it enhances the domestic economies by providing the liquidity to the business sector, such as financing the SME in the industry, circulating the fund in the market and creating more employments. For example, Finterra WAQFChain in Singapore collects cash waqf using the blockchain technology. The company builds on blockchain technology, and it allows waqf bodies, NGOs, Corporate CSRs, Trusts and other stakeholders with the opportunity to create or fund causes, submit project outlines/plans which are required to fund waqf and/or charitable projects and causes.

Each project has its own Smart Contract standard under the ERC-777. These Smart Contracts are placed into a fundraising project which only can be started once all due diligence requirements have been passed. After the fundraising is completed, the resulting Smart Contracts attached to the project are claimable by participants, as these digital assets are representative of a participant's stake in that specific waqf and/or charitable project or cause.

Noor Suhaida and Ismail (2021) conducted a qualitative study in Bangladesh which highlighted social enterprises' excellent practices that waqf institutions might adopt, notably in terms of sustainability and transparency. The Bangladesh Rural Advancement Committee's (BRAC) social enterprise is compared with three waqf entities: Malaysia's Larkin Sentral Property Berhad, Singapore's Warees Investment Ptd Ltd, and Indonesia's Pondok Modern Darussalam Gontor, where BRAC's successful accomplishment was used as a benchmark for waqf institutions. The results revealed that BRAC's long-term economic plan, as well as their governance, transparency, and social effects indicated the value of a capable management team, transparent reporting, and a disclosure database which is very important for any waqf organizations as they deal with public funds and trust. This indicates that these criteria are very significant to make sure that the waqf funds can be efficiently managed, therefore can be utilized for the benefit of many, including SMEs.

In Brunei, Basir and Besar (2021) discussed the potential, concerns, and constraints of supporting SMEs through *sadaqah*, waqf, or *zakat*. Brunei's Islamic Religious Council commended the use of Islamic social financing methods to promote SMEs. Brunei is one of the many nations affected by the COVID-19 pandemic. The findings from the study stated that ISF instruments have distinct qualities that enable them to be employed in a variety of situations and they are suited to the recipient's specific requirements. Combining waqf, *sadaqah*, and *zakat* in the effort to empower SMEs would be noteworthy since there is no one-size-fits-all approach to aid SMEs in their development and sustainability.

In Egypt, Miran (2009) discussed the policy of waqf in Eritrea's port city of Massawa. The study stated that waqf was frequently utilized to bypass Muslim inheritance rules in order to give land to families. The emergence of Hadhrami and Egyptian business people in Massawa was prompted by the city's expansion, owing to its proximity to the Red Sea and the building of the Suez Canal. To establish themselves in Massawa, entrepreneurs endowed urban property and tried to take command of waqf property. This is another method that can be used to help the entrepreneurs.

Kachkar (2016) studied the use of cash waqf to establish a model framework of a cash waqf micro-enterprise support model for refugees (CWMES-R) that covers the major issues of funding, advertising, and training. This study examined the reports and statistics from the United Nations High Commission for Refugees (UNHCR) which include countries all over the world, such as Iraq, Lebanon, and Egypt. To guarantee high participation, the model incorporates the use of temporary cash waqf. The money collected is subsequently divided into two groups, each with its own set of functions. Temporary cash waqf funds are used to assist refugee microenterprises, whereas perpetual cash waqf funds are invested in shariah-compliant investments. The revenues are utilized to fund the costs of operations. The framework can be adapted by other SMEs in other countries.

Ismail and Shaikh (2015) assessed the significance and utilization of waqf institutions in the Islamic economy. They suggest that waqf with large funds can also serve as a super-structure for the establishment of other commercial and social entities. In this context, Ahmed (2007) proposes a Waqf-based Islamic Microfinance organization that can provide microfinance and help the underprivileged build wealth. Furthermore, according to Ahmed (2007), Islamic banks can use money from late-payment penalties and other gains that they are unable to include in their income (such as interest earnings from treasury operations). Islamic banks can utilize these monies to establish a waqf and use them for microfinance activities. Microfinance can be provided by Islamic banks at cheaper operational and financing expenses. Most Islamic banks have a lot of cash on hand and have low advance-to-deposit ratios.

Next, a study by Mohd Thas Thaker et al. (2016) in Klang Valley, Malaysia, investigated the intention of micro-enterprises to use the integrated cash waqf microenterprise investment (ICWME-I) model. The model illustrated the partnership between cash waqf institutions and microenterprises where they jointly engage in business activities, and it is suitable for project and business financing. The theory of Reasoned Action was also adopted to identify factors that affected the intention to adopt the waqf model. The research was designed to test empirically the behavioral intention of micro-entrepreneurs to use the ICWME-I model. The attitude is defined as a participant's favorable or negative assessment of conducting the behavior. The subjective norm, on the other hand, relates to a person's sense of the social pressure placed on him or her to do, or not perform, a behavior. The findings showed that both attitude and subjective norms influenced the intention of micro-entrepreneurs to use the ICWME-I Model as one of the strategies to increase their access to finance.

Another finding from Mohd Thas Thaker (2018) is on the waqf model as a source of financing for micro-enterprises. The study found that the ICWME-I model was suitable as a financial service provider to micro-enterprises. The model involves the role of the donor towards cash waqf institutions, which will manage the fund and provide financial assistance for microenterprise, through the *musharakah mutanaqisah* partnership agreement. Apart from that, the attributes of micro-companies, the significance of sustainable funding, appropriate administration and management, legal concerns, and public awareness are all important variables that influence the ICWME-I model's long-term viability.

Meanwhile, a study by Shulthoni and Saad (2018) discussed both traditional fundraising such as *istibdal* (a substitution of waqf properties), *hukr* (monopoly), *ijaratayn* (dual payment lease) and modern fundraising such as venture philanthropy, the value-based capital model of waqf, and the social enterprise waqf fund (SEWF) models that can be utilized to generate and manage waqf. The SEWF model involves *waqif* to contribute waqf funds to *nazir*, whose background is from educational institutions or has social enterprise capabilities and is responsible to oversee the fund. The investment earnings will be allocated among beneficiaries, including educational institutions, with a maximum of 10 per cent going to *nazir*. The authors argued that since waqf aims for welfare enhancement, the SEWF model is appropriate to be used for sustainable waqf advancement and is considered as an innovation process in waqf fundraising and management.

In Indonesia, Anshori (2019) conducted an exploratory study to examine how Indonesia Waqf Venture (IWV), a venture institution funded by endowment funds, may help improve social welfare through Islamic-social entrepreneurship. The IWV combines the concept of social and commercial finance, involving the participation of the nation especially government, society, *ulama*, businessmen, and mass organization in economic development through a productive waqf economic model. It was found that IWV showed great promise as an Islamic investment alternative and a source of funding for entrepreneurs and investors. The study also found that demographics, productive and asset waqf, legal, and human resource development are all potentials of IWV.

Moreover, Alam et al. (2018) analyzed the factors leading towards the successful use of waqf in the social entrepreneurship context in major Muslim cities as a method for ensuring social welfare services in the past through literature review, as well as how the model may be recreated in current situations. The study found that the keys to moving forward are the foresighted or visionary entrepreneurs, advanced corporation-style management, employment of qualified human resources, and collaboration with philanthropy projects and community activists.

A study by Mar Iman and Haji Mohammad (2017) on how waqf-based entrepreneurship can be practiced in Malaysia found that Malaysia has a government waqf organization and waqf models, but the financial system, which involves the pressing need for the establishment of a waqf bank, has yet to mature. The waqf-based entrepreneurship concept includes philanthropists as the financers or contributors of input such as land, cash, or skills. The inputs are then used for activities that can produce valuable outputs such as profit income, asset value, and value appreciation. Privately owned commercial waqf management firms should be encouraged to participate. The study further suggested that waqf-based entrepreneurship can be utilized as an alternative socio-economic model for societal well-being.

In addition, Md Sahiq et al. (2016) conducted a conceptual study on waqf as an effective alternative resource to help young entrepreneurs in Malaysia succeed. The study aimed to offer waqf as a viable alternative to conventional funding. It focused on financial resources, and included two variables which are waqf, and resources based on a qualitative approach. The findings revealed that capital is the most important form of resource for young entrepreneurs seeking to grow and retain their enterprises. The study further stated that waqf has a lot of potential in providing access to funding enterprises and may act as a great instrument in the current tough economic environment. Another study, by Abdul Rahman et al. (2016), examined micro-entrepreneurs' intentions to adopt the Islamic micro-investment model (IMIM) in Bangladesh through a qualitative approach and the adaption of the theory of reasoned action. The IMIM portrayed a three-stage model developed from three different contracts, namely subsidized-*ijarah* contract (SIC), *mudarabah* contract, and *musharakah* contract, which were carried out by Islamic financial institutions. The institutions will then assist micro-entrepreneurs in need, and the output is expected to have a positive influence on poverty alleviation, faith satisfaction, employment, skills development, and inclusivity. Both behavioral belief and normative belief were found to be significant while attitude and subjective norm were insignificant. The findings demonstrated that the model matches the data in general and may be utilized to develop Islamic microfinance in Bangladesh. The IMIM model was focused on harnessing the role of the waqf philanthropic sector to empower micro-entrepreneurs.

A study by Ngah et al. (2018) suggests that waqf also can be used to promote entrepreneurship among students in higher educational institutions. They explored the impact of attitude, subjective norm, and perceived behavior control on waqf-based entrepreneurial intents among students, using the expanded Theory of Perceived Behavior (TPB). Aside from religious activities, one of the most common uses of waqf is to finance education. The findings supported that attitude, subjective norm, perceived behavior control, religion, and waqf awareness are all significant determinants of waqf-based entrepreneurial intention. Last of all, Khan (2019) conducted a study involving venture waqf in a circular economy in the effort to strengthen the influence of incorporated waqf organizations by pooling their resources to encourage responsible small companies that promote human growth, social service, and environmental and species protection. The findings suggest that an institutional framework for venture waqf be established to transform business paradigms from the existing waste-oriented linear economy to a zero-waste circular economy in the long run.

IMPACTS OF COVID-19 ON SMALL AND MEDIUM ENTERPRISES

The COVID-19 pandemic had different effects on different people. SMEs, particularly those managed by females, youth, minority groups, and immigrants, struggled the most in the private sector. According to a survey conducted by the International Trade Centre on the implications of COVID-19 on businesses, involving 136 countries, nearly 62 per cent of women-led small firms have been severely impacted by the crisis, as compared with the male-led businesses, while female-led businesses are 27 per cent more likely to fall victim to the pandemic (United Nations, 2021). Meanwhile, the OECD assessed the risks of a widespread liquidity crisis using a cross-sector sample of over one million enterprises in 16 European nations, spanning all industrial and non-financial sectors. The review found that policy action is necessary to avoid large bankruptcy. Without government's assistance, 20 per cent of the companies in the sample would run out of funds after one month, 30 per cent after two months, and 38 per cent after three months. More than half of the companies would suffer a cash difficulty if the lockout procedures were longer than seven months (SME Corporation, 2020a).

According to the International Trade Centre (ITC), the pandemic and accompanying containment efforts have had a substantial impact on 55 per cent of respondents in its COVID-19 Business Impact Survey, which included 4,467 enterprises from 132 countries. In comparison with roughly 40 per cent of large enterprises, over two-thirds of SMEs claimed their companies' operations are severely impacted. One-fifth of SMEs claimed they were on the verge of closing permanently (Kamal-Chaoui, 2020). In addition to enterprises, the outbreak has had a terrible impact on homes and what people owe, due to job losses and lower income. Microenterprises and SMEs, the private sector, the underprivileged, and the elderly are among the pandemic's most susceptible populations. The significant loss of employment in small enterprises, informal workers in temporary positions, gig economy employees, and the services sector all contribute to the pandemic's greater impact on households (SME Corporation, 2020a).

According to a report by OECD entitled "Tackling COVID-19 – Contributing to The Global Effort" in 2020, measures implemented by governments all around the globe are intended to solve immediate short-term issues while also encouraging SMEs to expand their operations. The majority of countries' policy-coordinating efforts are focused on health-related issues. SMEs are, however, specifically recognized in countries' coordinated efforts to reduce the economic impacts of the COVID-19 pandemic on enterprises, including SMEs. For example, in Australia, the government offered a stimulus package of AUD18 billion to help small businesses' cash flow; while the Japanese government introduced JPN1.6 trillion to grant zero-interest loans with no collateral to affected SMEs. Similarly, Hong Kong offers small and medium-sized businesses up to HKD2 million in loans under a financing guarantee plan with a total value of HKD20 billion, while in New Zealand, businesses having a turnover of NZD250,000 to NZD80 million will be qualified for financing of up to NZD500 000 over a three-year period (Safie, 2020).

COVID-19 is a pandemic that has had a substantial negative influence on both national and international economies. To avert an economic recession in Indonesia, the government has undertaken a number of initiatives aimed at increasing economic growth in the country. Airlangga Hartarto, the Coordinating Minister for the Economy, has stated that the third quarter of 2020 is a critical and tough period in the process of reviving the national economy. As a result, in the second semester, it is critical to optimize government expenditure. By 2020, the objective is to have Indonesia's total economic growth rate in the positive territory. The government promotes the development of micro and small enterprises, as well as micro and medium-sized firms, because they serve as the people's economic motor, which may help to improve economic growth and national economic recovery (Ministry of Investment, 2021).

According to the Institute for Development of Economics and Finance (INDEF), there are more than 64 million SMEs in Indonesia, with an estimated 60 million individuals employed by SMEs losing their jobs as a result of the COVID-19 pandemic's economic slump (*The Jakarta Post*, 2020). Consequently, the impact of the pandemic has sparked the need for digitalization among SMEs. For the past several years, Indonesian President Joko Widodo has repeatedly underlined the importance of digitization and digitalization for the country's economic development (Sakudo, 2021). The use of digital technology to restructure a business model and generate new income and value-producing opportunities is known as digitalization; it is the process of transitioning to a digital business (Gartner, 2021). The digital transformation process takes place as a result of these measures, and firms become a member of the digital economy in the process.

The pandemic has had a significant impact on Indonesia's economy. It experienced economic crisis, and the country's economy was anticipated to continue under strain in 2021, as the pandemic shows no indications of subsiding. According to Indonesia Resident Representative named Shimomura, in 2020, tourism, transportation, logistics, and the hotel industry are among the industries that have been affected the worst. Millions of Indonesians are also at risk of losing their jobs as the economy continues to deteriorate. The SMEs, which account for around 61 per cent of the country's Gross Domestic Product, will account for a large portion of the increase in unemployment as, in 2018, the sector employed 97 per cent of Indonesia's workforce.

A report by United Nations Development in 2020 highlighted key findings on the impacts of COVID-19 on SMEs in Indonesia. It was found that due to the pandemic, over half of the SMEs are having trouble sourcing raw materials, while nine out of ten SMEs saw a drop in the demands for their products and have difficulties in selling their goods. It was also revealed in the report that during the pandemic, almost 44 per cent of SMEs had joined online marketplaces or e-commerce channels such as Tokopedia and Shopee. Moreover, two-thirds of SMEs reported lower sales, and more than 80 per cent reported lower profit margins, and a decline in asset value was experienced by more than 53 per cent of SMEs. Challenges in terms of production, marketing, management of human resources, cost, and coping strategies were also faced by SMEs in Indonesia following the COVID-19 pandemic. Apart from that, most SMEs had their asset worth fall. More than 34 per cent of SMEs saw their asset value plummet by 20 per cent to 40 per cent. Another 30 per cent saw a 40 per cent to 60 per cent drop in the value of their assets. Not only that, as a result of the pandemic, several SMEs have also had to cut their workforce numbers.

The COVID-19 pandemic has encouraged the government to initiate several policies for SMEs in Malaysia. Initially identified as having spread to Malaysia on 25 January 2020, the COVID-19 pandemic was found to have spread there with reported cases remaining relatively small until a large sharp rise in cases was discovered in March 2020. As a result of the wide spread of the virus throughout the country, the Malaysian government announced the implementation of a Movement Control Order (MCO) from early March 2020 to the end of the month, which was later extended until April 2020. Consequently, given the unique set of conditions that SMEs are presently confronted with, the Malaysian government has implemented a few policies and programs to cushion and minimize the economic damage and disruptions caused by the COVID-19 pandemic. The following are some of the steps that have been implemented (SME Corporation, 2020a):

a. SMEs would benefit from a RM5 billion Special Relief Facility with an interest rate of 3.5 per cent.
b. Malaysian enterprises in the early-stage and growth-stage are the focus of a RM2 billion co-investment fund.
c. A RM700 million microcredit initiative with zero percent interest and no collateral for impacted firms has been launched.
d. A matching grant of RM500 million for the promotion of tourism.
e. The tourism and other impacted industries would get a RM100 million training matching grant.
f. RM50 million short courses in digital skills and highly skilled courses.
g. Employees' contributions to the Employees' Pension Fund (EPF) will be reduced from 11 per cent to 7 per cent from April 1 to December 31, 2020.
h. Employers can benefit from the Wage Subsidy Program, which helps them retain staff.

According to a report by Safie (2020), SMEs have less tolerance and adaptability in dealing with the cost disruptions and restricted supplies that have resulted from COVID-19, because they often depend on suppliers from countries that have had a higher number of COVID-19 incidents. While the fall in demand as a result of MCO has resulted in a reduction in output, the costs of idle labor and capital are borne more heavily by SMEs than by bigger corporations. Therefore, the policies and assistances were initiated by the government to cushion the impact and reduce the burden borne by SMEs in Malaysia.

The Asia Foundation conducted a survey in 2020 to assess the economic impacts to SMEs in Malaysia due to the pandemic. SMEs were found to be primarily concerned about their short-to-medium-term survival as a result of their operations grinding to a halt and no clear timeline for when situations will recover to usual; cash flow, credit management, and cost planning require

SMEs' greater attention and assistance. Micro and small firms are in worse shape than bigger businesses, as the majority of their owners do not have enough funds. Because Malaysian SMEs are predominantly focused on traditional industries and sub-sectors, it was also revealed that most Malaysian SMEs were unfamiliar with business digitalization and e-commerce even before the pandemic. Such SMEs should be assisted in expanding their horizons and learning about new business techniques, and the most important things that SMEs need from the state are grants, subsidies, and the continuation of loan moratoria (The Asia Foundation, 2021).

Furthermore, RM38.7 billion has been set aside in the annual national budget to support SMEs exclusively or in the same way as other firms. Access to funding, development of Bumiputera SMEs, human capital development, improving digitalization, technology and innovation, microenterprise development, market access, women entrepreneur development, and other tax policies are among the important activities (SME Corporation, 2020b). The Malaysian government responded to the threat of the coronavirus by enacting the PRIHATIN Economic Stimulus Package and the PENJANA Recovery Plan, which force SMEs to examine and reconsider their business practices in light of the "new normal". Therefore, to cope with the post-pandemic events, SMEs must equip themselves with necessary skills and innovative ideas to sustain themselves.

WAQF INITIATIVES TO HELP SMALL AND MEDIUM ENTERPRISES

In the months after the beginning of the COVID-19 pandemic, SMEs in developing Asian countries, including Malaysia and Indonesia, saw a significant drop in employment and sales income (Sonobe et al., 2021). The loss in employment was obviously particularly serious for non-permanent employees, but it was equally significant for permanent or regular employees. Despite significant disparities among nations, one-quarter to one-half of the sample SMEs had a temporary shutdown during this time, and one-third to two-thirds were experiencing cash shortages at the time of the study. In addition, as 67.8 per cent of SMEs claimed that they did not have any sales or income during the period of the MCO of COVID-19, statistics reveal that 53.4 per cent of SMEs would only be able to survive one to two months with full-time salary paid to the employees (Department of Statistics Malaysia, 2020). This is clearly a problem for SMEs during the pandemic, sustaining their businesses when their employment and revenue are badly affected.

In order to help SMEs to sustain their businesses during the pandemic, the role of Islamic financing tools such as waqf should be given attention. It was stated that waqf as a microfinancing remedy had been diminished and overlooked by the community as one of the major instruments in attempting to solve the economic crisis, particularly during COVID-19, and that it should be re-examined to highlight the importance of cash waqf as a source to help SMEs in Southeast Asia during this challenging period (Anuar et al., 2021). Existing programs, such as the Waqf Shares Scheme, could be evaluated to show how waqf can help SMEs, especially during the COVID-19 era, when any organization can set it up and serve as the waqf administrator, and contributors can buy waqf shares in the project in exchange for a cash waqf certificate as proof. Abdel Mohsin (2013) found that the Indonesian Waqf Scheme plan was a success, as it was able to fund poverty alleviation programs, medical benefits, and entrepreneur development. If cash waqf is extensively used to assist financing distressed SMEs on the verge of bankruptcy in Malaysia, a similar strategy might prove to be beneficial.

In addition, a report by Fanani et al. (2020) stated that the Productive Capital Waqf program by Global Wakaf-ACT in Indonesia has assisted almost 10,000 of those who are suffering to feed their families through many economic empowerment initiatives. For example, waqf for SMEs has successfully aided 3.7 thousand beneficiaries, while Productive Business Waqf has benefited over 100 business owners. This can be seen as an effective use of waqf to help SMEs in sustaining their businesses during the COVID-19 pandemic. Cash waqf is said to have a huge potential in Indonesia, the largest Muslim community in the world. Since cash waqf funds have been able to supplement governmental revenues in addition to taxes, *zakat*, and other sources of income, Indonesia no longer needs to rely on foreign creditor organizations for financing (Salleh et al., 2017). The role of cash waqf is not only to relieve their economic dependency from international creditors, but it may also serve as a catalyst for economic growth.

In early 2020, Bank Negara Malaysia introduced additional measures to further support SMEs affected by the COVID-19 pandemic. One of the programs implemented is iTEKAD, designed to support the B40 segment in the generation of sustainable income and achieve financial resilience. It utilized social finance (waqf, *zakat*, *sadaqah*), apart from educating and monitoring recipients' progress. A broader range of social finance instruments, such as cash waqf and social impact investment was later added, resulting in a blended finance feature, allowing low-income micro-entrepreneurs to acquire funds and grow their firms. The program's goal is to raise social finance contributions to provide initial funding and microfinance to eligible micro-entrepreneurs so they can start and expand businesses that produce long-term revenue. It was acknowledged that social finance has a lot of promise for facilitating more equitable and inclusive allocation of finances (Bank Negara Malaysia, 2022).

In this turbulent period, most SMEs are fighting to stay afloat. They must incur running expenditures, such as paying salaries and rental, during this difficult period, which is a challenge. Because most SMEs have limited capital, it has become an issue of survival for them. If the situation persists, they will not be able to survive. The role of Islamic financing in regard to the impact of the pandemic, especially on SMEs, still requires academic attention. However, in a broader scope of study, it was found that waqf is able to reduce the impacts of COVID-19 on the wellbeing of the society (Abdul Kareem et al., 2021). This indicates that Islamic finance via waqf can be used to alleviate the suffering and offer comfort to the community. Waqf institutions can help in this regard because they can provide funding to low-income individuals not only for their basic needs, but also for the start-up of SMEs, providing them with long-term sources of income.

The role of waqf in sustaining the business of SMEs during the COVID-19 pandemic requires further scholarly attention. As we know, waqf is a trust created when a donor permanently endows the stream of revenue generated by a property for a charitable purpose. Waqf and endowments can also be established for any philanthropic purpose and has traditionally taken the form of real estate, with land and structures being used for charity purposes including education, feeding the destitute, and providing religious rituals. Apart from that, it can also be used for more direct forms of financial inclusion, such as making cash payments to needy businesses or individuals from the endowment's proceeds or providing beneficiaries with means of livelihood, such as land, livestock, or equipment, through which they can participate in the financial economy (Ali et al., 2019). Hence, waqf, as a social finance tool, could help to lessen the pandemic's impact and effects.

The COVID-19 pandemic has a tremendous impact on all sectors in Malaysia, particularly the economic sector. Low-income individuals as well as SME businesses are the most affected since their revenue depends on the business itself. In response to the pandemic, Islamic finance institutions have been aggressively educating and reaching out to impacted clients about financial help services available. During the first half of 2020, a sum of RM120 billion in loans or financing to SMEs was granted, with far more applications being granted overall in 2020 than in prior years (Ghaffour, 2021). A study by Ali et al. (2019) stated that Fintech's crowdfunding and peer-to-peer (P2P) financing options give people and SMEs hope when they need money but do not qualify for traditional Islamic banking institutions.

In Indonesia, the Termination of Employment Relationship (PHK) is one of the impacts of the pandemic on the local businesses and subsequently, on the economy. Employees are faced with dismissal and companies are on the verge of bankruptcy. According to Rochmaniyah (2021), over 11,400 businesses have been terminated and workers laid off through PHK, with the overall number of employees impacted reaching over 1.9 million people. Similarly, SMEs industry in Malaysia lost a total of RM40.7 billion in 2020 due to the government's state-wide lockdown during the COVID-19 pandemic, indicating the suffering of entrepreneurs in sustaining their business. The Ministry of Entrepreneur Development and Cooperatives claimed that over 70 per cent of entrepreneurs have fallen into the B40 category, with limited funds and employment benefits (The Malaysian Reserve, 2021), and at least 150,000 SMEs are no longer in operation, causing 1.2 million job losses. Therefore, it is necessary to utilize an instrument to improve the efficacy of economic rehabilitation, such as the employment of waqf to help recover the impact of COVID-19.

ISF enables financial institutions to provide more practicable funding to SMEs. Waqf is gradually becoming mainstreamed via reforms and new innovations such as corporate waqf and short-term cash waqf. Waqf may also act as an equity investment where the incomes received are used to finance enterprises that offer a variety of social amenities. However, SMEs that are associated with a lack of credit history, a weak financial position, and an informal organizational setting would contribute to a high credit risk and this perception of credit risk and vulnerability may not match the financial institutions funding requirements (AIBIM, 2021). The CEO of Bank Islam Malaysia, Muazzam Mohamed stated that a much cheaper or lower rate should be ensured for SMEs in order to assist them get back on their feet after COVID-19, and using the social finance mechanism will not be free, but it will be substantially less expensive as compared with the traditional approach.

Based on a study by Ainol-Basirah and Siti-Nabiha (2020), waqf should be oriented towards more durable and feasible revenue generation investment for long-term socio-economic solutions, forming synergies with the *zakat* fund and other ISF mechanisms such as *sadaqah* and *qard-al-hasan*. Learning from the COVID-19 pandemic, it would be useful for SMEs to establish a waqf fund for crisis protection, to fulfil the immediate requirements of disadvantaged populations impacted economically. It is necessary to invest in sustainable forms of investments in order to grow the fund, which will then be handed to appropriate beneficiaries during times of crisis. Despite the fact that current waqf trends show a number of important waqf initiatives aimed at generating economic income, more innovations are undoubtedly required to boost this endeavor. As a result, waqf necessitates not just a sustainable pool of financial resources, but also the knowledge and expertise supplied by Muslim professionals to the waqf institutions in order to improve waqf efforts. Simultaneously, waqf institutions must be prepared to allow more collaborations for the sake of waqf development which benefits the entire society.

Apart from that, as the world continues to cope with the COVID-19 outbreak, the UN and the Islamic Development Bank (IsDB) announced an initiative to help finance efforts recover more quickly. The International Dialogue on the Role of Islamic Social Financing in Achieving the SDGs held in 2021, which will kick off vital talks on the role of Islamic social financing with world leaders and Islamic institutions, will be part of the effort. The President of IsDB also stated that waqf, *zakat*, *sadaqah*, and Islamic microfinance can contribute towards inclusive and robust development strategy. ISF, founded on the principles of faith and inclusivity, continues to be an important financing tool in the battle against food insecurity, in keeping with the SDGs of promoting social trust, partnership, and unity. The International Dialogue is urged to assess the idea of establishing a regional Islamic fund such as waqf to promote both immediate and long-term poverty reduction for the most vulnerable (Islamic Development Bank, 2021). This initiative may also be applied to businesses or SMEs affected by the COVID-19 crisis to help them sustain.

The former Prime Minister of Malaysia in 2020, Tan Sri Dato' Haji Mahiaddin Md. Yasin in his second announcement of the PRIHATIN Economic Stimulus Package, urged the use of ISF tools such as waqf (endowment), *zakat* (alms), and *sadaqah* (charity) in response to the increasing spread of COVID-19 and the threat it poses to Malaysia's economy. These tools are aimed at wealth redistribution and will be used to help micro-entrepreneurs gain access to capital and develop their entrepreneurship skills. They can be used to meet the basic necessities of the poorest and neediest people. These approaches aim to construct a social safety net by focusing on low-income populations, allowing for greater financial inclusion (World Bank Group, 2022). Therefore, more contributions can be made to help sustain SMEs during this COVID-19 pandemic with the emergence of ISF mechanisms such as waqf.

The allocation of RM500 million in the 'Sukuk Prihatin' has been announced as a means of rebuilding the economy. This Sukuk Prihatin program is sponsored by the government and used for several purposes, including funding SMEs. It is one of the supplementary options deployed to assist the government's pandemic post-recovery initiatives (*New Straits Times Business*, 2020). Hence, it may well be considered that the issuing of Sukuk is an option that can be utilized to alleviate the difficulties of micro-entrepreneurs and micro-businesses post-pandemic. The incorporation of resources into SMEs' capital can help lessen their financial obligations and thus, help them recover from the impact of COVID-19.

Since the outbreak of the pandemic, the government has implemented numerous aid programs and large stimulus packages covering individuals, families, and businesses (especially SMEs) to help the country's economy to recover. In the recent launching of 2022's Malaysian budget by the Prime Minister of Malaysia, Dato' Sri Ismail Sabri Yaakob, waqf's role as a wealth redistribution tool for the ummah's economic development will be bolstered in the future. Hence, the government will establish the Waqf SME Halal, Agriculture Waqf, and Disaster Waqf programs with RM10 million start-up capital to develop more agropreneurs and halal industry entrepreneurs, as well as to support them in the event of a disaster. This is a great initiative as the pandemic has impacted each one of us, especially those with a business to manage which incurs more cost.

On September 27, 2021, the Malaysian Prime Minister, YAB Dato' Sri Ismail Sabri Yaakob in his speech with regards to the Twelfth Malaysia Plan 2021–2025, highlighted that waqf will be developed in Malaysia as a method to explore monetary resources to finance enterprises and raise Bumiputra's equity. This is part of the efforts to further strengthen the Islamic economy. The waqf instruments will be strengthened through the establishment of a national waqf fund. The objectives are to generate more resources for entrepreneurs as well as to finance socio-economic development activities. To ensure more efficient waqf management, a National Waqf Master Plan 2021–2025 will also be implemented to help eradicate deep poverty, apart from being a financing source for entrepreneurial programs (Mohamad, 2021). Therefore, the development of ISF instruments, such as waqf, is in line with the Twelfth Malaysia Plan to empower the economy and national development.

WAQF AND SMALL AND MEDIUM ENTERPRISES: POSSIBLE SOLUTIONS?

This section highlights the possible solutions suggested by many researchers as well as industries related to waqf, which can be considered by countries to help the SMEs during and post pandemic.

The onset of the COVID-19 pandemic in 2020 has significantly altered business operations and the way people interact, as well as accelerated digital technology adoption. The pandemic has also exacerbated socio-economic inequalities and disparities. As a government that cares for its people, especially in times of crisis, the approach was implemented to mitigate the impact of the pandemic. The National Recovery Plan (NRP) was introduced in June 2021 as a phased strategy to transition out from the Movement Control Order (MCO) in terms of the movement of people as well as the reopening of economic and social sectors. The transition of phases will be determined through a data-driven approach based on three main indicators, namely the daily number of new cases, bed utilization rate in intensive care unit wards and percentage of the population that has been vaccinated (Economic Planning Unit, 2021).

According to Nik Azman et al. (2021), waqf could provide financing for small traders to restructure their businesses during economic crises encountered by Muslim nations. One of these is through proposing *musharakah* or *mudharabah* modes of financing. Cash waqf can be used to provide business capital for startups and for restructuring businesses. The profit earned in conducting business will be shared in an agreed ratio between both parties.

Ascarya (2021) conducted a study on the role of ISF instruments, including waqf, *zakat*, and *infaq*, during the COVID-19 pandemic in Indonesia's economic recovery. According to the study, 93.9 per cent of employment in SMEs were affected by the pandemic and, therefore, a conceptual framework was proposed to provide solutions through an Islamic perspective. The framework includes several approaches such as Umar al-Khattab's crisis management (Qureshi, 2019), poverty alleviation and inequality reduction (Yakubu & Aziz, 2019), and also the role of ISF instruments especially waqf, *zakat*, and *infaq*. Next, the study incorporated the conventional crisis management, by separating the recovery process into four categories as contents to be assessed:

1. Save lives – medical assistance such as quarantine, vaccines, healthy lifestyle.
2. Save households – social safety net such as secured employment, overcoming poverty, providing financing support.
3. Save businesses – financial assistance for micro, small and medium enterprises, subsidies, digital market set-up.
4. Save financial institutions – Islamic commercial and social finance (IICSF), assist in financial technology adoption, liquidity support.

The study also highlighted how SMEs endured a depletion of liquidity and even capital during the COVID-19 pandemic, as inadequate income from their enterprises has pushed them to spend their resources and capital to meet their fundamental requirements. These SMEs are in desperate need of assistance to sustain their companies, which might be provided through a variety of ISF instruments such as cash waqf, *zakat*, and *infaq*. Therefore, this study suggested an Islamic Economic Finance (IEF) approach to deal with the COVID-19 crisis, which comprises ISF that represents Muslim society's engagement and government assistance, focusing on the underprivileged, as well as SMEs, and spanning the health, home, business, and economic sectors.

Apart from that, Anuar et al. (2019) proposed a model framework to examine the role of Islamic microfinance as an instrument in facing the COVID-19 pandemic's impact on SMEs. It was further said that improvement of waqf can be done in terms of liquidity issues and consistency of donation by *waqif*. Figure 6.1 illustrates the waqf framework for SMEs, adapted from Allah Pitchay et al. (2015).

According to the study, the donor first contributes the funds using several accessible payment platforms, which then will be managed by waqf institutions who will identify potential small and medium enterprises in financial distress. Membership privileges will be granted to donors who make a specified

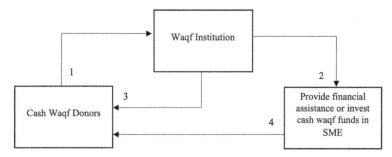

Figure 6.1   The waqf framework for SME

sum of cash waqf contributions and they will receive a preferential discount or accessibility to the services offered by the waqf-assisted SMEs. This model is significant as it improves donor trust in the waqf institutions, reduces the waqf institution's reliance on government funds to continue offering services, and stimulates wealth circulation from excess unit to deficient unit during COVID-19.

Furthermore, the *Qard-al-Hasan* Model is also identified to be a good way to boost economic growth and alleviate poverty, especially after the impact of COVID-19. *Qard-al-Hasan* is a voluntary loan in which the creditor has no intention of receiving a return on the principal. It is a no-interest-bearing charity loan with minimal intentions of capital return. *Qard-al-Hasan* is a potential alternative for reducing financial barriers by providing financial support to the disadvantaged, particularly those who do not have access to commercial microloans given the lack of collateral and a lack of affordability due to high funding costs. As businesses and individuals cope with the implications of COVID-19 on their earnings, the implementation of *Qard-al-Hasan* from banks might give some relief for them to get back on their feet until the situation stabilizes (Ali et al., 2021).

The *Qard-al-Hasan* Model has been successfully employed in the Iranian finance industry. The framework in Figure 6.2 is the *Qard-al-Hasan* system developed by Iran (adapted from Asgary, 2007).

Figure 6.2   The Qard-al-Hasan *model*

Based on the model, *Qard-al-Hasan* Funds (henceforth, QHFs) are a non-profitable organization wherein local residents establish a savings and lending society managed by a volunteer. The members, portrayed by A and B, contribute their money to the fund so that other members who require a short-term loan might receive assistance from it. A contributor can be a borrower at any time. Not only that, members also have the option of withdrawing some or all of their funds at any time. The depositor should not demand any amount other than his capital and the members are well-known and trustworthy to one another. Other expenses, such as stamps, stationery, transportation, and communication, are paid by certain QHFs by investing in business operations. Finally, the most important clause in the QHF agreement is that the debtors must pay the costs. Thus, the loan is not free, although the capital is.

According to Anuar et al. (2021), the QHF framework can be further established for Islamic banks to assist micro, small and medium enterprises with interest-free loans during the pandemic, since banks consistently want to help their target clients in times of emergency or liquidity crisis. These requirements are easily met by *Qard* services, which assist banks in establishing a strong and stable affiliation with their consumers. Further improvement in terms of selecting participants for the QHF program can be implemented to ensure stricter payment policies and reduce the level of risk. Therefore, even without an interest-based lending system, Islamic banking has provided useful instruments that can be developed and adapted to allow microfinance SMEs sustain in the current economy.

Moreover, Mohd Thas Thaker et al. (2021) proposed a conceptual framework of a cash waqf model for the advancement of SMEs in Malaysia. It is anticipated to offer SMEs ongoing support in the form of training and educational programs paid for by the cash waqf fund.

Based on the framework (Figure 6.3), cash waqf would be channeled to the cash waqf institution (CWI) by contributors (both public and private). The CWI serves as the mutawalli (manager) of the cash waqf fund under waqf legislation and would also be in charge of any investment decisions involving the cash waqf fund that has been established from the cash waqf collected from contributors. Second, the CWI would advertise HCD at a reduced cost by utilizing the cash waqf money to construct training centers with cutting-edge technology. Third, the CWI will provide skills development training programs and business-oriented educational short courses through the training facilities to assist SMEs in improving the effectiveness of their employees. Micro businesses would be required to pay a minimum fee at a subsidized rate in order to boost their participation. Finally, it is predicted that microenterprises would raise their productive output after getting the requisite training and skills from the CWI, leading to a rise in national wealth.

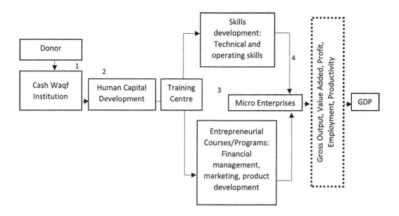

Figure 6.3   *Conceptual framework of the ICWME-I model (Mohd Thas Thaker et al., 2021)*

If properly implemented, the suggested concept might serve as a model for developing waqf funds in other nations, apart from overcoming many of the obstacles and constraints that come with building a long-term HCD facility. HCD is seen as any action taken to increase employees' productivity. As a result, the integrated cash waqf micro enterprise investment (ICWME-I) model is predicted to be able to adequately handle the issues of HCD for the economic advantage of micro entrepreneurs and other participants in general. This will be advantageous to Malaysia's overall SME sector growth wherein it assists young entrepreneurs in establishing long-term micro businesses. With the involvement of both the public and private sectors, this approach has the potential to help young entrepreneurs who are just starting out receive the essential training for HCD objectives, which will contribute to the creation of new job opportunities and the alleviation of poverty on a local level.

Next, Duasa et al. (2017) and Mohd Thas Thaker (2018) proposed the integrated cash waqf micro enterprise investment model to help improve micro enterprises' access to finance in Malaysia. The ICWME-I approach essentially provides financial assistance via a cash waqf fund. A participation contract between Islamic volunteer organizations, mainly waqf institutions and microfinance institutions, is also included (see Figure 6.4).

The first stage depicts the flow of funds from donors (both governmental and private sector) who make cash waqf contributions to the CWI with the goal of establishing a permanent waqf. The public can make a monetary waqf contribution by contributing money or purchasing waqf certificates from the

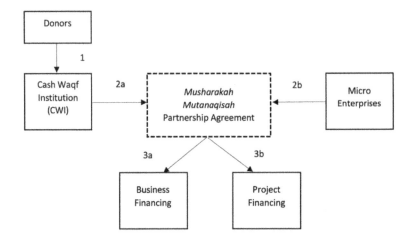

Figure 6.4   Conceptual framework of ICWME-I model (Mohd Thas
Thaker, 2018)

CWI, who becomes the fund's manager and is in charge of making all of the
fund's investment choices. As part of their CSR programs, businesses can
provide monetary waqf. The CWI can be considered as an independent body
or as a non-profit organization that falls under the jurisdiction of the Malaysian
SIRC or the private sector.

The second step is where the CWI would provide financial services by
engaging into *musharakah mutanaqisah* (diminishing partnership) agreements
with micro enterprises as shown by 2a and 2b in Figure 6.4. Both the CWI
and microenterprise would participate in business operations or buy real estate
or commercial companies together. The financier/and or the CWI's micro
enterprises' shares of ownership are divided into equal portions, with the idea
that the micro firms would progressively acquire their half of the property
through monthly payments, and CWI would profit from the arrangement. The
micro businesses would progressively become the sole owners of the property/
commercial enterprise towards the conclusion of the contract.

The same structure is appropriate for both commercial 3a and project
funding 3b in Figure 6.4. Machinery, land, power installation, and equipment,
are all examples of business finance. The building of retail lots and commercial
premises would be covered by project funding. The CWI does not demand
security under this approach, and no interest is imposed on the transaction. The
CWI, on the other hand, is obligated to undertake extensive due diligence on
potential micro companies relevant to their company. The model framework is

seen to be particularly beneficial in providing financial facilities to microenter-prises since it is able to offer an alternative for traditional financial institutions apart from assisting the government in lowering the costs associated with the growth of microenterprises.

The Sustainable and Responsible Investment (henceforth, SRI) sukuk framework was introduced in 2014 by the Securities Commission Malaysia to lay forth particular rules for the issuing of sukuk, encompassing the use of proceeds, qualifying SRI projects, disclosures, and the appointment of independent parties and reporting obligations. Sukuk refers to a certificate of ownership that proves possession of a real asset and is often seen as a type of Islamic bond that offers an alternative to traditional bonds (Shaikh & Saeed, 2010). The SRI Sukuk Framework is divided into four sections, namely:

a. Proceeds utilization – ensures that the proceeds raised are used on eligible SRI projects.
b. Project evaluation and selection process – ensures that internal methods for assessing and selecting eligible SRI projects are established by the issuer.
c. Proceeds management – ensures that eligible SRI projects must have their funds credited to a specified account or monitored in an acceptable manner by an issuer.
d. Reporting – ensures that the issuer gives necessary information to sukuk holders annually through a designated website.

The framework ensures that Islamic social finance can expand by making waqf-based investments more widely available. It includes the development of waqf assets as an SRI initiative, as well as the facilitation of the world's first waqf shares offering, since substantial opportunity for social progress, increased public benefits, and the distribution of wealth has been discovered in the establishment of waqf. Apart from that, the SRI projects include employ-ment creation by the SMEs and microfinance. Therefore, it would be beneficial if the framework is adopted in the SMEs sector.

The goal of SRI Sukuk Framework is to make it easier for SRI investors and issuers to create an ecosystem that encourages sustainable and responsible investing. The framework adheres to international norms and best practices, emphasizing the need of transparency when it comes to disclosure obligations. The waqf-featured fund framework would also expand the range of innovative Islamic capital market products available to the public and enable public access to Islamic funds that distribute all or part of their returns to socially beneficial activities through waqf (Securities Commission Malaysia, 2020).

This book aims to assist SMEs to formulate appropriate strategies and marketing using waqf for the sustainability of the business. The strategy is a necessity, especially because the government is aiming to promote a sustainable Islamic financial system. The COVID-19 pandemic in 2020 has changed organizational processes and the way people engage, as well as hastening the use of digital technology. Inequalities and gaps in socio-economic status have been worsened by the outbreak. Despite the fact that the concept and structure of waqf have been established for decades, waqf has been afflicted by several problems, including poor asset management, governance, transparency, accountability, and inefficiency. Due to the surge in continual innovations and disruptions occurring in the Islamic financial and technical terrain, waqf has recently been obliged to adjust itself in order to remain relevant. Due to the fact that waqf assets are managed by a trust or foundation, their ability to attract money for development may be limited.

One of the successful solutions related to waqf, particularly to deal with the COVID-19 pandemic, is offered by Finterra, an organization dedicated to building the next generation of blockchain. Finterra, a prominent technology-based firm that provides blockchain-based Islamic applications that address global concerns, was founded in 2017 and has offices in Malaysia, Singapore, Hong Kong, the United Arab Emirates, and India, with intentions to expand further into Africa and the Middle East. Finterra aims to provide a "Social Solution for Blockchain" that fosters community growth and promotes the widespread acceptance of groundbreaking blockchain technology. Its ecosystem includes core banking, digital banking, and blockchain solutions, all of which were created with the goal of narrowing the gap between consumers, merchants, and financial institutions. According to the Merriam-Webster dictionary, blockchain is defined as a large decentralized, publicly accessible network that contains a digital database containing information, such as financial transaction records, that can be used and shared at the same time. Finterra helps create optimized business models by offering a comprehensive set of blockchain-based solutions for traditional businesses.

WAQFChain is the flagship product of Finterra that offers efficient methods in creating and managing cash waqf funds, as well as providing a path to develop waqf assets through smart contract multi-chain ecosystems. Waqf is often regarded as the most prominent form of Islamic charities. It is a philanthropic foundation by which long-term assets that create revenue flows may be developed and conserved, and it stands out as one of the biggest accomplishments of Islamic civilization. These assets, in turn, aid in the production and generation of income for the benefit of society as a whole. It is based on blockchain technology and allows waqf bodies and other stakeholders to develop or finance causes, as well as submit project outlines and plans that are necessary to support waqf and/or charitable projects and causes.

Finterra claims that their WAQFChain offers transparency in all financial transactions by storing them immutably and publicly for the review of stakeholders. Due to the fact that Smart Contracts are backed by Block chain consensus, there is also no room for corruption. The Smart Contracts under the ERC-777 standard are applied on each project where these Smart Contracts placed in a crowdfunding project can only begin if all due diligence pre-determined criteria have been met. Participants can claim the resulting Smart Contracts tied to the project after the crowdfunding is done, as these digital assets represent a participant's ownership in that specific Waqf project or cause. Fundraising through WAQFChain contributes towards the advancement of Islamic Social Finance and charitable causes. Apart from that, the platform is able to unlock the liquidity that has been locked up in waqf assets, while enabling all parties involved in the ecosystem to be on the same platform, or, as they called it, an integrated system. Figure 6.5 portrays the waqf platform and how it works.

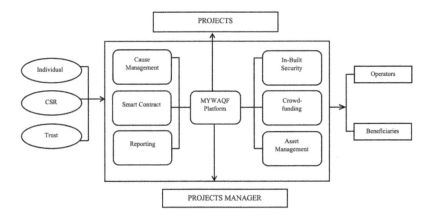

Figure 6.5   MYWAQF platforms by Finterra

Figure 6.5 explains how blockchain can support raising capital for waqf development using the Finterra MYWAQF Platforms. Users (individuals, trusts, CSR) set an account and deposit funds into the Finterra Waqf Chain, which is stored in an Islamic Bank Trust Account. Profit sharing applies to all monies in the trust account. Depositors can see the causes that have been established on Finterra such as Waqf Charitable Causes, Islamic Investment Opportunities, and Islamic Peer-to-Peer Lending. In order to increase crowd participation, Islamic financial institutions promote Islamic investment alternatives in the Finterra Waqf Chain, while SMEs advertise Islamic trade credit. Smart Contracts allow users to participate in charity, Islamic investment, and peer-to-peer lending. Within the Finterra Waqf Chains (blockchain), users may monitor their participation and transactions, ensuring immutability and transparency.

For a waqf project, a development project paper is written, and it is reviewed and approved by an independent auditor. After that, a licensed fund manager is hired to launch an Initial Coin Offering (ICO) to raise funds for the development of the specific waqf development project by selling crypto tokens to pre-qualified investors all over the world. The ICO process employs the idea of crowdfunding, raising small sums of money from the large public to fund a project. The waqf chain, which is constructed on top of the Finterra block chain, launches the token in exchange for the requisite capital. The fund management chooses a firm to begin building and developing the project after the capital is raised. The fund management hires an asset manager to operate and maintain the asset when construction is completed. Any revenue or income earned by the asset is paid to the fund manager. Depending on the investment instrument utilized and the underlying terms and conditions, the collected revenues or income are then shared with the investors. The operators for MYWAQF platforms are Finterra technologies, partnering banks, and the partnering waqf foundation, while the beneficiaries include the areas of healthcare, education, religion, refugees and the environment.

Blockchain technology is expected to maintain waqf-related initiatives on a global scale. It has a lot of promises because of its low cost, attention on quality assurance, high traceability, ability to conduct peer-to-peer transactions while securing data from manipulation, and the fact that it virtually minimizes error rates. Therefore, the global community should acknowledge the enormous influence of blockchain technology, which will undoubtedly manage waqf-related initiatives in a secure and proper manner. With Finterra pioneering the blockchain technology in waqf, it suggests that the technology could be the key to improving the current state of waqf efforts throughout the world.

To conclude, waqf can serve as the medium of wealth distribution to society as a whole in eradicating poverty and it can be the channel to enhance socio-economic services. The waqf system has played a significant socio-economic role throughout the history of Islamic civilization. It was the fact that essential services were all provided at no cost whatsoever to the government. This has certainly had many important implications and effects on the overall economy. By providing essential services to society at zero cost to the state, the waqf system can significantly contribute towards the ultimate goals of every modern economy: a massive reduction in government expenditure. This, in turn, lowers the need for government borrowing, and a reduction in the budget deficit. In addition, it also leads to a reduction in interest rates, and, thereby, cuts out a major impairment for private investment and growth.

Finally, waqf will enhance the country's overall economic progress through voluntary donations made by the people in the society.

> ...you who believe! Spend of the good things which you have (legally) earned, and of that which We have produced from the earth for you. (Surah Al Baqarah: Ayat 267)

Bibliography

Abdel Mohsin, M. I. (2012). Waqf-shares: New product to finance old waqf properties. *Banks and Bank Systems*, 7(2), 72–78.

Abdel Mohsin, M. I. (2013). Financing through cash-waqf: A revitalization to finance different needs. *International Journal of Islamic and Middle Eastern Finance and Management*, 6(4), 304–321. https://doi.org/10.1108/IMEFM-08-2013-0094

Abdel Mohsin, M. I., Dafterdar, H., Cizakca, M., Alhabshi, S. O., & Abdul Razak, H. (2016). *Financing the development of old waqf properties: Classical principles and innovative Practices around the World*. Springer.

Abdelfattah, N. A., Elsiefy, E., Youssef, A., & Ragheb, M. (2021). A conceptual comparison between conventional endowment funds and Islamic waqf funds. *International Journal of Economics, Commerce and Management*, IX(2), 317–340.

Abduh, M. (2019). The role of Islamic social finance in achieving SDG number 2: End hunger, achieve food security and improved nutrition and promote sustainable agriculture. *Al-Shajarah*, 2019 (Special Issue Islamic Banking and Finance 2019), 185–206.

Abdul Kareem, I. A., Mahmud, M. S. bin, Elaigwu, M., & Abdul Ganiyy, A. F. (2021). Mitigating the effect of Covid-19 on the society through the Islamic social finance. *The Journal of Management Theory and Practice* (JMTP), 2(1), 57–61. https://doi.org/10.37231/JMTP.2021.2.1.83

Abdul Karim, S. (2010). *Contemporary Shari'ah Structuring for the Development and Management of Waqf Assets in Singapore*. Durham University. http://etheses.dur.ac.uk/778/

Abdul Rahman, R., Muhammad, A. D., Ahmed, S., & Amin, F. (2016). Micro-entrepreneurs' intention to use Islamic micro-investment model (IMIM) in Bangladesh. *Humanomics*, 32(2), 172–188. https://doi.org/10.1108/H-02-2016-0020

Abdul Razak, S. H. (2019). Mosque tourism in Malaysia: A marketing perspective. *International Journal of Social Science Research*, 1(2), 108–120.

Abdul Razak, S. H. (2020). Zakat and waqf as an instrument of Islamic wealth in poverty alleviation and redistribution: Case of Malaysia. *International Journal of Sociology and Social Policy*, 40(3-4), 249–266. https://doi.org/10.1108/IJSSP-11-2018-0208

Abdullah, M. (2018). Waqf, sustainable development goals (SDGs), and Maqasid al-Shariah. *International Journal of Social Economics*, 45(1), 158–172. https://doi.org/https://doi.org/10.1108/IJSE-10-2016-0295

Abdullah, A., & Yaacob, H. (2012). Legal and Shariah issues in the application of Wakalah-waqf model in takaful industry: An analysis. In JIBES University (Ed.), *International Congress on Interdisciplinary Business and Social Science 2012 (ICIBSoS 2012)* (Vol. 65, pp. 1040–1045). Jakarta, Indonesia: Elsevier. https://doi.org/10.1016/j.sbspro.2012.11.239

Abu Bakar, M., Ahmad, S., Salleh, A. D., & Md Salleh, M. F. (2020). Waqf and sustainable development goals (SDGs): A Critical review from Malaysia perspective. *Journal of Critical Reviews*, 7(13), 2362–2385.

Ahmad, I., & Hasan, H. (2018). *Dynamic Efficiency of Malaysian Public Waqf-A bench-marking analysis*. Kota Bharu, Kelantan: UMK Press.

Ahmad, A., Kashif-ur-Rehman, & Asad Afzal, H. (2011). Islamic banking and prohibition of riba/interest. *African Journal of Business Management, 5*(5), 1763–1767.

Ahmed, H. (2007). Waqf-based microfinance: Realizing the social role of Islamic finance. In *International Seminar: Integrating Awqaf in the Islamic Financial Sector* (pp. 1–22). Singapore.

AIBIM (2021). Islamic social finance a viable way to assist MSMEs. https://aibim.com/news/islamic-social-finance-a-viable-way-to-assist-MSMEs

Ainol-Basirah, A. W., & Siti-Nabiha, A. K. (2020). The roles of Islamic social finance in the era of post-Covid-19: Possible prospects of waqf institutions for economic revival. *International Journal of Industrial Management, 7*(1), 1–8. https://doi.org/10.15282/ijim.7.0.2020.5747

Alam, M. M., Shahriar, S. M., Said, J., & Monzur-E-Elahi, M. (2018). Waqf as a tool for rendering social welfare services in the social entrepreneurship context. *Global Journal Al-Thaqafah, 2018*(January), 87–98. https://doi.org/10.7187/gjatsi2018-06

Al-Buti, I. M. S. R. (2009). The glorious legislation of endowments in the history of Islamic civilization and looking for means to bring it back. In A. AlSharbini (Ed.), *The Book of Endowment* (pp. 117–132). Kuala Lumpur: IBFIM.

Al-Haddad, S. H., & Suleman, U. (2021). Awqaf-led Islamic social finance: Innovative solutions to modern applications. In Mohd Ma'sum Billah (Ed.), *Awqaf-led Islamic Social Finance* (pp. 83–99). Oxon: Routledge. https://doi.org/10.4324/9780429356575

Ali, K. M., Hassan, M. K., & Abd Elrahman Elzahi, S. A. (eds) (2019). *Revitalization of waqf for socio-economic development*. Palgrave Macmillan.

Ali, S. A. M., Arshad, A., & Ibrahim, I. (2021). Relief measures of Islamic finance combating adverse impacts of Covid 19 in Malaysia: An analysis. *International Journal of Law, Government and Communication, 6*(24), 116–134.

Allah Pitchay, A., Mydin, M., Kameel, A., & Saleem, M. (2015). Factors influencing the behavioral intentions of Muslim employees to contribute to cash-waqf through salary deductions. *Journal of King Abdulaziz University, Islamic Economics, 28*(1). Retrieved from https://ssrn.com/abstract=3065257

Ambrose, A. H. A. A., Aslam, M., & Hanafi, H. (2015). The possible role of waqf in ensuring a sustainable Malaysian federal government debt. In *International Accounting and Business Conference 2015, IABC 2015* (Vol. 31, pp. 333–345). Elsevier B.V. https://doi.org/10.1016/s2212-5671(15)01205-8

Annuar, A. (2020). Covid-19: After MCO, survey finds nearly 70pc SMEs lost half income. *Malay Mail*. March 27, 2020. Retrieved from https://www.malaymail.com/news/malaysia/2020/03/27/covid-19-after-mco-survey-finds-nearly-70pc-smes-lost-half-income/1850688

Anshori, M. (2019). The potential of Indonesia waqf-venture in increasing welfare through Islamic-socialpreneurship. *Opción: Revista de Ciencias Humanas y Sociales*, (21), 53-68.

Anuar, A., Bahari, Z., Doktoralina, C., Indriawati, F., & Nugroho, L. (2019). The diversity of waqf implementations for economic development in higher education. *IKONOMIKA*, 13–34.

Anuar, N. S. K., Shobri, A. N., & Abdullah, M. S. (2021). Islamic microfinance as an instrument in facing Covid-19 pandemic impact on micro, small, and medium enterprises (MSMEs). https://www.researchgate.net/publication/

349423823_islamic_microfinance_as_an_instrument_in_facing_covid
- 19_pandemic_impact_on_micro_small_and_medium_enterprises_msmes

Artini, L. G. S., & Ni Luh Putu, S. S. (2020). Comparison of SME stock portfolio and manufacturing company performance in the Indonesian, Indian and Chinese stock markets. *Journal of Economic and Administrative Sciences, 37*(2), 209–237. https://doi.org/https://doi.org/10.1108/JEAS-04-2019-0044

Ascarya, A. (2021). The role of Islamic social finance during Covid-19 pandemic in Indonesia's economic recovery. *International Journal of Islamic and Middle Eastern Finance and Management.* 20, 2021. https://doi.org/10.1108/IMEFM-07-2020-0351

Asgary, A. (2007). Informal microfinance institutions: Case of Qard Hasan funds in Iran. In *Non-Bank Financial Institutions: Islamic Alternatives.* Islamic Research and Training Institute.

Ayuba, M. N., Noordinb, N., Mohamed Sawal, M. Z., Mat Hassan, S. H., & Taha, M. M. (2020). Analysis of the administration and management of people's religious schools in Kedah, Malaysia. *International Journal of Innovation, Creativity and Change, 13*(4), 1121–1134.

Azganin, H., Kassim, S., & Auwal Adam, S. (2021). Proposed waqf crowdfunding models for small farmers and the required parameters for their application. *Islamic Economic Studies.*

Azha, L., Baharuddin, S., Sayurno, Salahuddin, S. S., Afandi, M. R., & Hamid, A. (2013). The practice and management of waqf education in Malaysia. *Procedia – Social and Behavioral Sciences, 90*(InCULT 2012), 22–30. https://doi.org/10.1016/j.sbspro.2013.07.061

Bakar, R. (2018). Cash waqf for education: Prospects and challenges. *Journal of Emerging Economies and Islamic Research, 6*(2), 1–4.

Bank Negara Malaysia. (2007). *Resolutions of the Securities Commission Shariah Advisory Council.* Kuala Lumpur: Securities Commission.

Bank Negara Malaysia. (2022). Malaysian Financial Sector. Retrieved from https://www.bnm.gov.my/islamic-banking-takaful

Basir, Khairul Hidayatullah & Besar, M. H. A. (2021). Unlocking Islamic social finance to assist micro small medium enterprises in Brunei Darussalam. In *COVID-19 and Islamic Social Finance* (1st ed., p. 14). Routledge.

Bilal Khan, M., Ahmad Ghafoorzai, S., Patel, I., & Damkar, M. S. (2021). Waqf based Islamic fintech model for agriculture sector of Indonesia. *International Journal of Business Ethics and Governance, 4*(1). https://doi.org/10.51325/ijbeg.v4i1.61

Borham, A. S., & Mahamood, S. M. (2013). Wakaf korporat Johor Corporation dan sumbangannya dalam memenuhi tanggungjawab sosial Islam di Malaysia: Satu Tinjauan. *Journal of Techno Social, 5*(2), 61–77.

Budiman, M. A. (2014). *The Significance of Waqf for Economic Development. Munich Personal RePEc Archive.* Retrieved from https://mpra.ub.uni-muenchen.de/81144/1/MPRA_paper_81144.pdf

Candra, H., & Ab Rahman, A. (2010). Waqf investment: A case study of Dompet Dhuafa Republika, Indonesia. *Shariah Journal, 18*(1), 163–190.

Che Man, N., Abd Wahab, N. A., Ab Hamid, N., & Nordin, R. (2019). Potential of waqf instrument in tourism industry in Malaysia. *Journal of Islamic Philanthropy & Social Finance, 1*(1), 38–54.

Cizakca, M. (1998). Awqaf in history and its implications for modern Islamic economies. *Islamic Economic Studies, 6*(1), 43–70.

Cizakca, M. (2021). Waqfs in the Philippines. Retrieved November 26, 2021, from https://islamicmarkets.com/education/waqfs-in-the-philippines

Deloitte Indonesia. (2021). P2P cash waqf crowdfunding platforms: The next frontier for Islamic philanthropy in Indonesia. *Deloitte Indonesia Perspectives*, (February).

Department of Economic Planning and Statistics. (2021). *Laporan Kiraan Awal Jumlah Penduduk Brunei Darussalam Tahun 2021*. Brunei Darussalam. https://deps.mofe .gov.bn/SitePages/Population.aspx

Department of Statistics Malaysia (2020). *Report of Special Survey on Effects of COVID-19 on Economy & Individual – Round 2*. 10–24 April 2020.

Department of Statistics, Ministry of Trade & Industry, R. of S. (2020). *The Census of Population 2020: Statistical Release 1 Demographic Characteristics, Education, Language and Religion*. Retrieved from https://www.singstat.gov.sg/-/media/files/ publications/cop2020/sr1/cop2020sr1.pdf

Dinar Standard. (2021). *Global Islamic Fintech Report. Salaam Gateway*. Retrieved from https://cdn.salaamgateway.com/special-coverage/islamic-fintech-2021/Global -Islamic-Fintech-Report-2021-Executive-Summary.pdf

Dipta, W. (2017, June). *Indonesia SME Strategy*. ILO/OECD Workshop for Policy Makers on Productivity and Working Conditions in SMEs.

Dorloh, S. (2015). Reviewing the law for Muslim affairs in enhancing the waqf institution in Thailand: A way forward. *The Journal of Muamalat and Islamic Finance Research*, *12*(2), 33–40.

DOSM. (2021). *SMEs Performance 2020*. DOSM.

Doumani, B. (1998). Endowing family: Waqf, property devolution, and gender in greater Syria, 1800 to 1860. *Comparative Studies in Society and History*, *40*(1), 3–41. doi:10.1017/S001041759898001X

Duasa, J., Asmy, M., Mohd, B., & Thaker, T. (2017). Proposed integrated cash waqf investment model for micro enterprises in Malaysia: An empirical analysis. *Journal of Islamic Philanthropy & Social Finance*, *1*(2), 2590–3942.

Economic Planning Unit. (2021). *Twelfth Malaysia Plan: 2021-2025 A Prosperous, Inclusive, Sustainable Malaysia*. Percetakan Nasional Malaysia Berhad.

Fanani, A., Rosyada, M. A., Syauqoti, R., Muhammad, N., & Rosyida, N.N. (2020). Proposed waqf based food barn for food security through cash waqf: Case study in global waqf-act, Jipang, Blora, Indonesia, *U-Go Healthy 2020*, March 29, Pacitan, Indonesia, DOI 10.4108/eai.29-3-2020.2315361

Gabil, H., Bensaid, B., Tayachi, T., & Jamaldeen, F. (2020). The need for shari'ah-compliant awqāf banks. *Journal of Risk and Financial Management*, *13*(4), 76. https://doi.org/10.3390/jrfm13040076

Gamidullaeva, L. A., Vasin, S. M., & Wise, N. (2020). Increasing small- and medium-enterprise contribution to local and regional economic growth by assessing the institutional environment. *Journal of Small Business and Enterprise Development*, *27*(2), 259–280. https://doi.org/https://doi.org/10.1108/JSBED-07 -2019-0219

Gartner. (2021). *Definition of Digitalization - IT Glossary | Gartner*.

Ghaffour, A. R. (2021). Maximising Islamic finance for inclusive growth: From crisis to opportunity. *Opening remarks, Deputy Governor of the Central Bank of Malaysia, Launch of the World Bank Islamic Finance Reports*, 7 October 2020. https://www .bnm.gov.my/-/deputy-governor-s-opening-remarks-at-the-launch-of-the-world -bank-islamic-finance-reports

Global Islamic Finance Report. (2015). Waqf and Islamic banking and finance: The missing link. *Global Islamic Finance Report 2015*, 113–130.

Haji Puteh, F. (2019). Potensi wakaf terhadap pertanian di negara Brunei Darussalam. *Jurnal Ekonomi Sakti, VII*(2), 94–106. Retrieved from http://jes.stie-sak.ac.id/index .php/103044/article/view/197/112

Harris, E. (2018). Statement at the global symposium on the role of Micro, Small and Medium Enterprises (MSMEs) in the achievement of the Sustainable Development Goals | United Nations. Department of Economic and Social Affairs, United Nations. Retrieved from https://www.un.org/ru/desa/statement-global-symposium -role-micro-small-and-medium-enterprises-msmes

Hasan, S. (2011). Role of waqf in enhancing Muslim small and medium enterprises (SMEs) in Singapore. In *8th International Conference on Islamic Economics and Finance* (pp. 1–50).

Hasan, H. (2016). Efficiency determinants of Malaysian public waqf in a dynamic environment. (Doctoral dissertation, Universiti Teknologi MARA, Malaysia).

Hasan, H., & Ahmad, I. (2017). *Taxonomy of Waqf and the Economy.* Kota Bharu, Kelantan.

Hassan, M. K., Rabbani, M. R., & Abdulla, Y. (2021). Socioeconomic Impact of COVID-19 in MENA region and the role of Islamic finance. *International Journal of Islamic Economics and Finance (IJIEF), 4*(1). https://doi.org/10.18196/ijief.v4i1 .10466

Hennigan, P. C. (2004). *The Birth of a Legal Institution: The Formation of the Waqf in Third- century A.H. Ḥanafī Legal Discourse.* Brill.

Hubur, A. (2019). Productive waqf management: A case study of Brunei Darussalam. *International Journal of Islamic Business, 4*(1), 65–87.

Husin, A. (2020). *Impact of Waqf Specific Characteristics, Macroeconomic Conditions and Regulatory Determinants on Waqf Institution Efficiency in Malaysia.* [Doctoral dissertation, Universiti Teknologi MARA.]

Hussin, R. (2021). An overview of the regulatory framework for waqf implementation in higher educational institutions in Malaysia. *Journal of Legal, Ethical and Regulatory Issues, 24*(1).

Hussin, R., Kader, S. Z. S. A., Manshor, N. M., Roslim, S., & Sirat, I. M. (2021). Good governance practices for waqf in Malaysian Higher Education Institutions (HEIs). *Academy of Strategic Management Journal, 20*(2), 1–6.

Ibrahim, D., & Ibrahim, H. (2013). Revival of waqf properties in Malaysia. In *The 5th Islamic Economics System Conference (iECONS 2013)* (pp. 4–5). Kuala Lumpur, Malaysia: Faculty Economics and Muamalat.

IGILife. (2021). *Wakalah-waqf model.* IGI Life Insurance Limited.

Ikram, I. (2021). *Malaysian SMEs' GDP shrank 7.3% in 2020, more than overall economy's contraction of 5.6%.* The Edge Markets.

Indonesian Ministry of National Planning. (2018). *Indonesia Islamic Economic Masterplan 2019-2024.* (Deputy of Economy Indonesian Ministry of National Development Planning, Ed.), *Indonesian Ministry of National Development Planning.* PT Zahir Syariah Indonesia. Retrieved from http:knks.go.id

Internal Finance Corporation. (2010). *Scaling-Up SME Access to Financial Services in the Developing World.* Internal Finance Corporation.

Islamic Development Bank. (2021). *Development Effectiveness Report 2021.* Jeddah, Kingdom of Saudi Arabia.

Islamic Finance Council UK. (2021). *Islamic Finance: Shariah and the SDGs – Thought Leadership Series Part 4* (Issue October). Islamic Finance Council UK.

Islamiyati, I., Hendrawati, D., Musyafah, A., Hakimah, A., & Marom, R. (2021). A juridical study of land waqf in Indonesia in realizing the rule of law. *Proceedings* of the 2nd International Conference on Law, Economic, Governance (ICOLEG 2021), 29–30 June 2021, Semarang, Indonesia. https://doi.org/10.4108/eai.29-6 -2021.2312621

Ismail, M. 'Izzuddin. (2021). *Sustainability of Tourism Industry in Malaysia: An Application of waqf model*. Universiti Teknologi MARA.

Ismail, M. I., Ismail, S., Zahari, M. S., & Mohd Pauzi, N. F. (2021). Sustainability of tourism industry in Malaysia: An application of waqf model. *International Journal of Business and Economy, 3*(1), 127–138.

Ismail, N. A., Omar, I., Abu Bakur, M. N. R., Suhaili, N. A., & Mansor, R. (2016). Cross-sector partnership: Leveraging the cost of waqf higher education institutes (HEIs). In S. Kayadibi & S. Alimova (Eds.), *International Symposium on Waqf and Higher Education* (pp. 160–168). Kuala Lumpur: Centre for Islamic Economics (CIE).

Ismail, C. Z., Salim, N. J., & Hanafiah, N. J. A. (2015). Administration and management of waqf land in Malaysia: Issues and solutions. *Mediterranean Journal of Social Sciences, 6*(4 S2), 613–620. https://doi.org/10.5901/mjss.2015.v6n4s2p613

Ismail, A. G., & Shaikh, S. A. (2015). Using waqf as social safety net funding public infrastructure. *Munich Personal RePEc Archive*. https://mpra.ub.uni-muenchen.de/ id/eprint/68751

Jalil, A., & Mohd Ramli, A. (2014). Conceptualisation of corporate waqf. In *Seminar Waqf Iqlimi 2014* (pp. 310–321). Retrieved from http://ddms.usim.edu.my:80/jspui/ handle/123456789/9866

Kachkar, O. (2016). *Towards Developing an Integrated Cash-Waqf Microenterprise Support for Refugees Model to Enhance their Livelihood and Self-reliance*. International Islamic University Malaysia. Retrieved from chrome-extension:// efaidnbmnnnibpcajpcglclefindmkaj/http://studentrepo.iium.edu.my/bitstream/ 123456789/3675/1/t11100350525OmarKachkar_SEC_24.pdf

Kahf, M (1998, March 2–4). *Financing the development of awqaf property* [Conference presentation] 1998 Seminar on Development of Awqaf, Islamic Research and Training Institute (IRTI), Kuala Lumpur, Malaysia.

Kamal-Chaoui, L. (2020). *Rescuing SMEs from the COVID Storm: What's Next?* The OECD Forum Network.

Kamaruddin, M. I. H., & Mohd Hanefah, M. (2021). An empirical investigation on waqf governance practices in waqf institutions in Malaysia. *Journal of Financial Reporting and Accounting, 19*(3), 455–473. https://doi.org/10.1108/JFRA-03-2020 -0055

Khan, T. (2019). Venture waqf in a circular economy. *ISRA International Journal of Islamic Finance, 11*(2), 187–205. https://doi.org/10.1108/IJIF-12-2018-0138

Ku Hanani, K. H. (2021). Possibilities on concept of waqf mechanism in developing the entrepreneurship activities. *International Journal of Zakat and Islamic Philanthropy, 3*(1), 74–81.

Kuwait Finance House (n.d.). Maqasid Shariah. https://www.kfh.com.my/malaysia/ personal/about-us/islamic-banking-services/maqasid-shariah.html

Mahadi, N. F., Mohd. Zain, N. R., & Muhammad Ahmad, S. (2021). Achieving the sustainable development goals: The role of Islamic social finance towards realizing financial inclusion in the unprecedented Covid-19. In *Handbook of Research on Islamic Social Finance and Economic Recovery after a Global Health Crisis*. https:// doi.org/10.4018/978-1-7998-6811-8

Majlis Ugama Islam Singapura (2020). Wakaf. Retrieved from https://www.muis.gov .sg/wakaf/Understanding-Wakaf/Wakaf-Assets

Malaysian Accounting Standards Board. (2014). *MASB Research paper Waqf*. http://www.masb.org.my.

Mahendhiran, S. N. (2020). Going digital and more incentives can mitigate Covid-19 impact. *The Star*. March 22, 2020. https://www.thestar.com.my/news/focus/2020/03/22/going-digital-and-more-incentives-can-mitigate-covid-19-impact

Mar Iman, A. H., & Haji Mohammad, M. T. S. (2017). Waqf as a framework for entrepreneurship. *Humanomics*. https://doi.org/https://doi.org/10.1108/H-01-2017-0015

Md Saad, N., Mhd Sarif, S., Osman, A. Z., Hamid, Z., & Saleem, M. Y. (2017). Managing corporate waqf in Malaysia: Perspectives selected SEDCs and SIRCs. *Shariah Journal*, *25*(1), 91–116.

Md Sahiq, A. N., Ismail, S., Bakri, M. H., Abd Rahman, N. H., & Husin, A. (2016). A conceptual study on waqf young entrepreneur model: An alternative model for financing enterprises in Malaysia. *American Scientific Publishers*, *22*. https://doi.org/10.21098/jimf.v1i2.533

Medias, F., Pratiwi, E. K., & Umam, K. (2019). Waqf development in Indonesia: Challenges faced by Muhammadiyah Waqf Institutions. *Economica: Jurnal Ekonomi Islam*, *10*(2), 239–254. https://doi.org/10.21580/economica.2019.10.2.3333

Midgley, J. (2008). Microenterprise, global poverty and social development. *International Social Work*, *51*(4), 467–479. https://doi.org/10.1177/0020872808090240

Ministry of Foreign Affairs. (2018). Mid-term Review of the Eleventh Malaysia Plan 2016–2020 (new priorities and emphases). Putrajaya, Malaysia: Percetakan Nasional Malaysia Berhad. Retreived from http://www.epu.gov.my

Ministry of Investment. (2021). Strengthening MSMEs as drivers of national economic recovery | Invest Indonesia. Ministry of Investment.

M. Nasir, F., & Patria, N. (2021, July). A page from history: Demystifying waqf for transforming Indonesia. *The Jakarta Post*. Retrieved from https://www.thejakartapost.com/academia/2021/01/28/a-page-from-history-demystifying-waqf-for-transforming-indonesia.html

Miran, J. (2009). Endowing property and edifying power in a Red Sea port: Waqf, Arab migrant entrepreneurs, and urban authority in Massawa, 1860s–1880s. *The International Journal of African Historical Studies*, *42*(2), 151–178.

Mohamad Al-Bakri, Z. (2020). Spearheading waqf culture. Retrieved July 24, 2021, from https://zulkiflialbakri.com/spearheading-waqf-culture/

Mohamad, M. H. (2021). Waqf puts prospect of home ownership within our reach. *New Straits Times*, October 22, 2021. https://www.nst.com.my/opinion/columnists/2021/10/738649/waqf-puts-prospect-home-ownership-within-our-reach

Mohamad, N. A. (2018). A study on the socio-economic roles of waqf ahli (family waqf) in promoting family security and a sustainable family economy. *IIUM Law Journal*, *26*(1), 141–160.

Mohamed Nor, S., & Yaakub, N. I. (2015). Transformation of the role of waqf in Malaysia. *Advanced Science Letters*, *23*(1). https://doi.org/10.1166/asl.2017.7232

Mohd Arshad, M. N., & Mohamed Haneef, M. A. (2016). Third sector socio-economic models: How waqf fits in? *Institutions and Economies*, *8*(2), 75–93.

Mohd Hanefah, H. M., Jalil, A., Mohd Ramli, A., Sabri, H., Nawai, N., & Shahwan, S. (2011). Financing the development of waqf property: The experience of Malaysian and Singapore. *The Journal of Muamalat and Islamic Finance Research*, *8*(1), 89–104.

Mohd Noor, M. I., Mohd Noorii, F. N., & Aziz, F. Y. (2019). Application waqf in shariah compliant hotel industry. *Journal of Fatwa Management and Research*, *16*(2), 127–137.

Mohd Shukri, N. D. S., Ahmad Zamri, S. N., Muneeza, A., & Ghulam, H. (2019). Waqf development in Marawi city via issuance of perpetual waqf sukuk. *International Journal of Management and Applied Research*, *6*(2), 68–80.

Mohd Thas Thaker, M. A. (2018). A qualitative inquiry into cash waqf model as a source of financing for micro enterprises. *ISRA International Journal of Islamic Finance*, *10*(1), 19–35.

Mohd Thas Thaker, M. A., Amin, M. F., Mohd Thas Thaker, H., Khaliq, A., & Allah Pitchay, A. (2021). Cash waqf model for micro enterprises' human capital development. *ISRA International Journal of Islamic Finance*, *13*(1).

Mohd Thas Thaker, M. A., Mohammed, Mustafa Omar Duasa, J., & Abdullah, M. A. (2016). The behavioral intention of micro enterprises to use the integrated cash waqf micro enterprise investment (ICWME-I) model as a source of financing. *Gadjah Mada International Journal of Business*, *18*(2), 111–130.

Mohd Zain, N. R., Mahadi, N. F., & Noor, A. M. (2019). The potential in reviving waqf through crowdfunding technology: The case study of Thailand. *Al-Shajarah*, *2019* (Special Issue Islamic Banking and Finance 2019), 89–106.

Muhammad, M. Z., Char, A. K., Yasoa', M. R. bin, & Hassan, Z. (2009). Small and Medium Enterprises (SMEs) competing in the global business environment: A Case of Malaysia. *International Business Research*, *3*(1).

Mustafa, G., Aslam, M. A., & Nazeer, S. (2021). Muslim community of Thailand in historical perspective. *Zia-e-Tahqeeq*, (20), 65–80. Retrieved from https://www.researchgate.net/publication/350108697_muslim_community_of_thailand_in_historical_perspective/citation/download

Najim, N. F. (2021). Developing cash waqf model as an alternative financing for social enterprises to support decent work and economic growth in Indonesia. *Turkish Journal of Islamic Economics*, *8*(Special Issue), 195–217. https://doi.org/10.26414/a2759

New Straits Times Business (2020). RM500mil Prihatin sukuk for Malaysians to help rebuild economy. *New Straits Times*, June 7, 2020. https://www.nst.com.my/business/2020/06/598686/rm500mil-prihatin-sukuk-malaysians-help-rebuild-economy

Ngah, R., Salleh, Z., & Abidin, Z. Z. (2018). Exploring micro enterprises business performance through entrepreneurial orientation, knowledge sharing and innovation. *Management & Accounting Review*, *18*(2), 93–106. https://ir.uitm.edu.my/id/eprint/31191/

Nik Azman, N. H., Masron, T. A., & Ibrahim, H. (2021). The significance of Islamic social finance in stabilising income for micro-entrepreneurs during the Covid-19 outbreak. *Journal of Islamic Monetary Economics and Finance*, *7*(1), 115–136. https://doi.org/10.21098/jimf.v7i0.1307

Noor Suhaida, & Ismail, S. F. A. (2021). Social enterprise and waqf. In Mar Burki, Toseef Azid, & D. R. Francis (Eds), *Foundations of a Sustainable Economy* (1st ed.). London: Taylor & Francis.

Nu Htay, S. N., Salman, S. A., & Soe Myint @ Haji Ilyas. (2013). Integrating zakat, waqf and sadaqah: Myint Myat Phu Zin clinic model in Myanmar. *Tazkia Islamic Finance and Business Review*, *8*, 170–185.

Obaidullah, M., & Khan, T. (2008). *Islamic Microfinance Development: Challenges and Initiatives. Islamic Development Bank*. Jeddah: King Fahd National Library Cataloguing-in-Publication Data. https://doi.org/10.2139/ssrn.1506073

OECD. (2013). Working party on SMEs and Entrepreneurship (WPSMEE) – Financial technology (Fintech) SMEs. Paris: OECD.

OECD. (2016). *Entrepreneurship at A Glance*. Paris. OECD. https://doi.org/http://dx .doi.org/10.1787/entrepreneur_aag-2016-en.

OECD (2020). *Tackling COVID-19 – Contributing to the Global Effort*. OECD.

Omar, A. J., Wan Yusoff, W. Z., Mohamad, M., & Wan Zahari, W. A. M. (2018). Current issue in corporate waqf in Malaysia. *Advanced Science Letters, 24*(5), 3045–3051. https://doi.org/10.1166/asl.2018.11315

Omar, H. H., Ab Rahman, A., Mazlan, A. R., Abu Bakar, A., & Abd. Kadir, S. (2013). The structuring for development and management waqf properties in Malaysia. *Journal of Human Development and Communication, 2*, 45–59.

Osman, S., Mat, I., & Ahmad, J. (2015). Unlocking value of waqf property using Hibah Mudharabah: A case study of commercial buildings in Kedah, Malaysia. *International Journal of Development Research, 5*(5), 4294–4299.

Pertiwi, R. S., Hadi Ryandono, M. N., & Khofidotur Rofiah, A. (2019). Regulations and management of waqf institutions in Indonesia and Singapore: A Comparative Study. In *the 2nd International Conference on Islamic Economics, Business, and Philanthropy (ICIEBP)* (pp. 766–783). KnE Social Sciences. https://doi.org/10 .18502/kss.v3i13.4246

Pew Research Centre. (2009). *Mapping the Global Muslim Population*. Pew Research Centre, Washington, USA. https://www.pewresearch.org/religion/2009/10/07/ mapping-the-global-muslim-population/

Qureshi, F.A. (2019). Crisis Management Policies of Caliph "Umar Bin Khattab". Published November 8, 2019.

Qurrata, V. A., Narmaditya, B. S., Seprillina, L., & Hussain, N. E. B. (2019). The implementation and development of productive waqf in Indonesia: Case at Malang Islamic Hospital. *Humanities and Social Sciences Reviews, 7*(4), 533–537. https:// doi.org/10.18510/hssr.2019.7471

Rahmad, H., & Duriat, F. (2020, July). Singapore's Islamic social finance and Halal businesses. *Islamic Finance News*, (July), 26–27.

Rahman, N. A., Yaacob, Z., Busneti, I., & Tambunan, T. (2016). A comparative study on development of SMEs and policies in Indonesia and Malaysia. *International Journal of Small and Medium Enterprises and Business Sustainability, 1*(4), 74-103.

Rochmaniyah, I. (2021). Dampak Pandemi Covid-19 Terhadap Penyerapan Tenaga Kerja Dan Pendapatan Usaha Mikro Kecil Menengah Kedai Kopi Di Sentra Kopi Sudimoro Kota Malang Skripsi.

Rosadi, A., Effendi, D., & Busro. (2013). The Development of Waqf Management through Waqf Act in Indonesia (Note on Republic of Indonesia Act Number 41 of 2004 on Waqf). *Journal of Institutional Economics, 9*(4), 469–490.

Rozali, E. A., & Alias, N. A. B. (2019). Administration of waqf fund in Fatih Hospital, Istanbul (1470–1824). *Malaysian Journal of History, Politics & Strategic Studies, 46*(July), 112–130.

Rusydiana, A. S., Sukmana, R., & Laila, N. (2021). Waqf on education: A bibliometric review based on Scopus. *Library Philosophy and Practice, May*.

Saad, A. I. (2019). The corporate waqf in law and practice. *Berkeley Journal of Middle Eastern & Islamic Law, 10*(1), 1–22. https://doi.org//doi.org/10.15779/ Z38NC5SC93

Sadeq, A. M. (2002). Waqf, perpetual charity, and, poverty alleviation. *International Journal of Social Economics, 29*(1/2), 135–151

Safie, S. (2020, March 30). SMEs: Policy responses to the Covid-19 pandemic in Malaysia. *Department of Statistics Malaysia*, pp. 1–4. Retrieved from

https://www.dosm.gov.my/v1/uploads/files/6_Newsletter/Newsletter 2020/
DOSM_BPPD_2-2020_Series-59.pdf

Saidon, R., Alam Selangor Malaysia Mohd Afandi Mat Rani, S., Dani Muhamad, M., Alam, S., Hayati Ishak, A., & Afandi Mat Rani, M. (2019). Examining the practice of waqf-based education in Indonesia. *International Journal of Civil Engineering and Technology (IJCIET)*, *10*(2), 814–819.

Sait, S. and Lim, H. (2006). *Land, Law and Islam: Property and Human Rights in the Muslim World.* London, UK: Zed Books.

Sakudo, M. (2021). *The New Normal: Digitalization of SMEs in Indonesia.* Published February 9, 2021. Retrieved July 1, 2021, from https://www.asiapacific.ca/publication/new-normal-digitalization-msmes-indonesia

Salarzahi, D. H., Armesh, H., & Nikbin, D. (2010). Waqf as a social entrepreneurship model in Islam. *International Journal of Business and Management*, *5*(7), 179–187. https://doi.org/10.5539/ijbm.v5n7p179

Salleh, N., Nor, A. H. M., & Roni, M. S. M. M. (2017). Waqf-based endowment and entrepreneurial intention among students in institutes of higher learning. In M. Cingula, M. Przygoda, & K. Detelj (Eds), *23rd International Scientific Conference on Economic and Social Development*. Madrid, 15–16 September. *Economic and Social Development. Book of Proceedings*, pp. 701–709.

Securities Commission Malaysia. (2014). *Waqf Assets: Development, Governance and the Role of Islamic Capital Market.* Perpustakaan Negara Malaysia.

Securities Commission Malaysia. (2019). Impact investing as an extension to the Islamic economy. *Proceedings of the SC-OCIS Roundtable 2019, March.*

Security Commission Malaysia. (2020). 2020 In review – Driving sustainability. *Malaysian Islamic Capital Market*, *15*(2).

Shaikh, S., & Saeed, S. (2010). Sukuk bond: The global Islamic Financial Instrument, *Business Islamica*, *1*(11).

Shamsiah, A. K. (2010). *Contemporary Shari'ah Structuring for the Development and Management of Waqf Assets in Singapore.* Durham University. http://etheses.dur.ac.uk/778/

Shulthoni, M., & Saad, N. M. (2018). Waqf fundraising management: A conceptual comparison between traditional and modern methods in the waqf institutions. *Indonesian Journal of Islam and Muslim Societies*, *8*(1), 57–86. https://doi.org/10.18326/ijims.v8i1.57-86

Siraj, S. A. (2012). An empirical investigation into the accounting, accountability and effectiveness of waqf management in the state Islamic religious council (SIRCs) in Malaysia. [Doctoral dissertation, Cardiff Business School, University, Cardiff University.]

SME Corporation. (2020a). COVID-19: Impact on businesses and SMEs-Global, Regional & National Perspectives. SME Corporation

SME Corporation. (2020b). *SME Development Policies, Initiatives and Programmes.* 168–183. SME Corporation.

SME Corporation Malaysia. (2021a). *SME Corporation Malaysia - Micro Enterprises.* SME Corporation Malaysia.

SME Corporation Malaysia. (2021b). *SME Corporation Malaysia - SME Definition.* SME Corporation Malaysia.

Sonobe, T., Takeda, A., Yoshida, S., & Truong, H. T. (2021). The impacts of the COVID-19 pandemic on Micro, Small, and Medium Enterprises in Asia and their digitalization responses. In *ADBI Working Paper Series* (No. 1241; Issue 1241). https://doi.org/10.2139/ssrn.3912355

Sukmana, R. (2020). Critical assessment of Islamic endowment funds (Waqf) literature: Lesson for government and future directions. *Heliyon*, *6*(10), e05074. https://
doi.org/10.1016/j.heliyon.2020.e05074

Tambunan, T. (2008). SME development in Indonesia with reference to networking,
innovativeness, market expansion and government policy. In H. Lim (Ed.), *SME in
Asia and Globalization*, ERIA Research Project Report 2007-5, pp. 99–131.

Tambunan, T. (2015). *ASEAN Micro, Small and Medium Enterprises Towards AEC*.
Lambert Academic Publishing (LAP).

Tambunan, T. (2019). Recent evidence of the development of micro, small and medium
enterprises in Indonesia. *Journal of Global Entrepreneurship Research*, *9*(1). https://
doi.org/10.1186/S40497-018-0140-4

The Asia Foundation. (2021). *Enduring the Pandemic: Surveys on The Impact of
Covid-19 to the Livelihoods of Malaysian SMEs & Workers*. 1–49.

The Jakarta Post. (2020). Gojek supports 100,000 SMEs move online. *The Jakarta
Post*.

The Malaysian Reserve (2021). MSME sector suffered RM40.7b losses in 2020. *TMR
Media Sdn Bhd*. Published July 29, 2021. Retrieved from https://themalaysianreserve
.com/2021/07/29/msme-sector-suffered-rm-40-7b-losses-in-2020-49-at-risk-of
-collapse-by-oct-2021/

The World Bank Group. (2016). *Global Report on Islamic Finance: Islamic Finance –
A Catalyst for Shared Prosperity?* World Bank Group. https://doi.org/10.1596/978
-1-4648-0926-2

The World Bank Group, INCEIF, & ISRA. (2019). *Maximizing Social Impact through
Waqf Solutions*. www.worldbank.org/en/country/malaysia%7C www.inceif.org
%7C www.isra.my%0A©May

UDA Holdings Berhad. (2021). History. Retreived from http://www.uda.com.my/index
.php/home/beginnings

United Nations. (2021). *Micro-, Small and Medium-sized Enterprises Day*. United
Nations.

United Nations Development Programme Report (2017). Waqf for financing the
Sustainably Development Goals (SDGs). https://www.id.undp.org/content/
indonesia/en/home/presscenter/articles/2017/12/11/untapped-great-potential-of
-waqf-for-sustainable-development-in-indonesia-.html

United Nations Development Programme Report (2020). Impact of COVID-19 pandemic on MSMEs in Indonesia. *LPEM, FEB, Universitas. Indonesia*. https://www
.undp.org/sites/g/files/zskgke326/files/migration/id/INS-Report-Impact-of-COVID
-19-Pandemic-on-MSMEs-in-Indonesia.pdf

United Nations Saudi Arabia. (2021). *The Role of Awqaf in Achieving the SDGs and
Vision 2030 in KSA*. Saudi Arabia. https://saudiarabia.un.org/en/146145-role-awqaf
-achieving-sdgs-and-vision-2030-ksa

US Department of State. (2018). *Timor-Leste 2018 International Religious Freedom
Report*. United States of America. https://www.state.gov/reports/2018-report-on
-international-religious-freedom/vietnam/

US Department of State. (2020a). *Laos 2020 Financial technology (Fintech)*. https://
www.state.gov/wp-content/uploads/2021/05/240282-LAOS-2020-Financial technology (Fintech).pdf

US Department of State. (2020b). *Vietnam 2020 International Religious Freedom
Report*. https://www.state.gov/wp-content/uploads/2021/05/240282-VIETNAM
-2020-Financial technology (Fintech).pdf

US Department of State (2021). *Philippines 2020 International Religious Freedom Report.* United States of America. https://www.state.gov/reports/2020-report-on -international-religious-freedom/philippines/

van Slyke, D. M., & Newman, H. K. (2006). Venture philanthropy and social entrepreneurship in community redevelopment. *Nonprofit Management and Leadership, 16*(3). https://doi.org/10.1002/nml

Wan Ismail, W. M. (2020). Significance of technology to cash waqf collection: Application of Unified Theory Acceptance and Use of Technology (UTAUT). *International Journal of Academic Research in Business and Social Sciences, 11*(1), 777–788. https://doi.org/10.6007/ijarbss/v11-i1/8994

Wasiuzzaman, S., Nurdin, N., Abdullah, A. H., & Gowrie, V. (2020). Creditworthiness and access to finance: a study of SMEs in the Malaysian manufacturing industry. *Management Research Review,* 293–310. https://doi.org/https://doi.org/10.1108/ MRR-05-2019-0221

World Bank Group (2022). *Small and Medium Enterprises (SMEs) finance, improving SMEs' access to finance and finding innovative solutions to unlock sources of capital.* Retrieved November 11, 2021, from https://www.worldbank.org/en/topic/ smefinance

World Islamic Economic Forum. (2014, October). The WIEF Chronicles: Banking on the Growth of Waqf. *World Islamic Economic Forum Foundation,* (13).

World population review. (2021). https://worldpopulationreview.com/

Yaacob, H. (2013). Waqf history and legislation in Malaysia: A contemporary perspective. *Journal of Islamic and Human Advanced Research, 3*(6), 387–402.

Yaacob, H., Yaacob, A., Basir, K. H., & Ali, Q. (2020). Enabling legal environment of Islamic finance and social finance in Brunei Darussalam: A demand for improvement (pp. 186–195). *IGI Global.* https://doi.org/10.4018/978-1-7998-3452-6.ch013

Yakubu, A., & Aziz, A. H. A. (2019). The role of waqf in economic sustainability and poverty reduction. *International Journal of Academic Research in Business and Social Sciences, 9*(12), 708–714.

Yoshida, E. (2019). FinTech-enabled cash waqf: Effective intermediary of social finance. In *Revitalization of Waqf for Socio-Economic Development: Vol. I* (pp. 43–58). Palgrave Macmillan, Cham. https://doi.org/10.1007/978-3-030-18445 -2

Zain, N. S., & Muhamad Sori, Z. (2020). An exploratory study on Musharakah SRI Sukuk for the development of waqf properties/assets in Malaysia. *Qualitative Research in Financial Markets, 12*(3), 301–314.

Zulu-Chisanga, S., Chabala, M., & Mandawa-Bray, B. (2021). The differential effects of government support, inter-firm collaboration and firm resources on SME performance in a developing economy. *Journal of Entrepreneurship in Emerging Economies, 13*(2), 175–195. https://doi.org/https://doi.org/10.1108/JEEE-07-2019 -0105

Index